FURY

A Soldier's Journey

Joe Myles

Published by Salt Water Media
29 Broad Street, Suite 104
Berlin, MD 21811
www.saltwatermedia.com

Cover design by Salt Water Media with image used courtesy of Unsplash user, David Beale.

AUTHOR'S NOTE

This book of recollections is written for my sons and grandchildren with the help and encouragement of my love, Patsy, and is dedicated to the brave men I spent my time with in the Army during the Vietnam years, who left the safety and security of their homeland to fight an enemy in a distant country. They were willing to sacrifice their lives fighting for their country, so that their family and friends could enjoy their freedom.

Disclaimer: This is my recollection of events, and have related them to the best of my knowledge.

TABLE OF CONTENTS

Lying there in a pool of my blood on an Olive Drab canvass hammock stacked three high in the H-1D Huey helicopter, I was wondering if this was how my life would end. Would the nineteen years spent preparing for my future, studying, learning, and testing in school have been wasted time? Would the years serving in the Civil Air Patrol, and participating in team sports all be erased, as if it never happened? What about the career path I already chose to follow in civilian life, and of course all of the extra efforts and training to excel in "this man's Army." Does that go away too? Now this! Does it end this way? No, it can't end this way!

THE JOURNEY BEGINS

On a typically warm Maryland Fall night in 1967, a full year after our graduation from high school, I was sitting in a circle of chairs with four of my closest buddies – a scene that had been repeated regularly many times over the past few years. While we were still in High School our conversations usually centered around what we planned to do the following day, what we were going to eat for a late night snack, or offer advice to each other on how to negotiate through relationships with our girlfriends. We had all the answers then.

Graduation was behind us now and our situations had changed. We were now Junior College students attending classes at night while working at various entry level jobs at minimum wage, during the day. Our incomes were just enough to pay for car insurance (for those fortunate enough to have a ten year old drivable vehicle), or to pay a fair percentage of the insurance on our parents policies! I didn't fall in either category. My wages went toward supplementing my family's living costs, an occasional Royal Burger or Mighty Mo treat, or the time I spent eight dollars and change for a pair of Chuck Taylor low tops.

Recently our late night problem solving sessions had turned to the topic of the Vietnam war since we all were at the prime age for the Draft. And for now we were all exempt from the Draft as long as our grades stayed above passing, and we maintained our student status. The Draft Board assigned every man reaching the age of eighteen and registering, a number that was placed in a big drum. When it was determined additional men needed to be called into service, numbers would be drawn from that drum, and those men would be drafted into the service.

The decision making process I had on my plate concerned my high school girlfriend, Margy, with whom the discussion of marriage was a daily event. The Vietnam war was preventing us from being able to plan our future, since being called into the service after completing the two year Junior College was a real possibility. We all struggled with decision making at that age, and during those times it was all so new for us, and it seemed each choice we made would be permanent. It was difficult enough deciding what careers we would be pursuing let alone trying to guess when we would be able to start them. Tough time for a kid to outline such big, multiple life choices that would significantly affect his future.

Time has a way of answering the big questions and at times force the direction as to which path you should follow, and in January of 1967 I was presented with two choices.

My girlfriend's father offered to sponsor me to apprentice as a machinist at the Government Printing Office where he was employed. And within a few days of that offer, her brother told me there was an opportunity to join the International Union of Elevator Constructors. Each offer possibility had its own advantages and perks. I didn't know much about government careers except that employment was very secure all the way until time of retirement, but I knew even less about Union careers, except that they had been formed to protect children from being exploited from working them at very young ages for very little money. I bounced back and

12

forth during the next several days trying to decide which choice would be best for me. After all this was a job I would be working at for the rest of my life. At that age it didn't occur to me that whatever my choice, I could always change my mind and change careers.

The Elevator trade was the choice I made to follow, but the Draft was still there looming and threatening to disrupt my life.

I started working in the Elevator trade January 10, 1967 as an apprentice or Helper as it was called in the trade, learning how to install elevators and escalators. The company's name was Montgomery Elevator, a large international company based in Moline, Illinois. I could have been assigned to work at any job site in the entire Washington metropolitan area for my very first day of work, but as luck would have it I was told to report to the location of the new Iverson Mall being constructed. The mall was being built in Hillcrest Heights, Maryland – only two blocks from my house, and the Mall was being built on the vacant land that my buddies and I used to play sandlot baseball. How great was that! I was able to walk to work and could even run home for lunch if I didn't want to pack a lunch and bring it with me. But wait, it gets better. Since the job site was located in the 1st Zone, determined by a measurement from the District of Columbia's benchmark, I received something called zone pay. The zone pay was extra money for traveling further than the workers in downtown Washington, D.C., this had been negotiated years prior by the Union and Elevator companies. Life was good.

I continued working in the elevator trade over the next few months, showing up every weekday ready to work, and the work day start was very early. I looked forward to going to work because I was learning new skills and receiving the side benefit of a good work-out and getting in better physical shape.

Reporting to the job site on a particularly cold day, our Foreman gathered everyone together and told the mechanics to pack their tools and lock the job down. I asked my mechanic what that all meant and explained we were going on strike. How about that, I was going to be able to participate in the very first strike the trade union ever had. He said do not report for work the following day. I informed him I would rather work instead of striking and would be coming in for work the next day as usual. After he had a good laugh at my expense, he explained I really did not have a choice in the matter – everyone had to strike!

Well it turns out my timing was not the very best, not that I had any control on whether to strike or not to strike, but I did have some control on whether to get married, or not to get married. Unfortunately just prior to the untimely announcement of the Strike I made an announcement of my own, giving my girlfriend an engagement ring making her my fiancee.

Now being on strike does create some hardships since a person on strike is not allowed to apply for unemployment benefits. I had to find another job or two to replace the higher income I had gotten used to with Montgomery Elevator. All of a sudden I had real financial responsibilities: car payments, auto insurance, Union dues, and of course engagement ring payments.

REPLACEMENT INCOME

I started submitting job applications immediately everywhere in my area. I wasn't seeking any particular type of work, just anything that would bring in some cash during the strike. Among the businesses I interviewed with was the Marriott Restaurant in the Marlow Heights Shopping Center which featured buffet type dining. I presented myself to the manager as an experienced cook, which was the truth, although I did try to appear more accomplished in the culinary field than I actually was. The manager probably seeing through my experience story, offered to start me at the work station cleaning pots and pans. He said after a time I could move up to cleaning the dishes, and then go to food preparation at the salad station before advancing to the food preparation line. His philosophy was that was what he did when he started in the business, and worked his way up to manager. He felt everyone else should have to climb the same ladder. The manager's rationale made sense for all of the applicants seeking a job position that lacked training and experience – but not me! I thanked him for his time and offer, but said that I must decline his offer to start at the pot and pan station. With that said, I left.

After a few days went by I landed a daytime job with Brinner's Rental starting at 7 am, and finishing at 4 pm. I also got a night job with the Scot's Gas Station from 11 pm until 7 am.

Brinner's Rental was a Mom and Pop operation, and I was basically the only employee. The store rented many types of gas powered lawn and mechanical equipment: fold up six foot tables and chairs, along with a multitude of party and wedding service dishware and accessories. My duties were to help the customers find what they needed for various occasions, or power equipment they needed for certain projects. After they found what they wanted I would process their rental items, then help them load everything into their vehicles. When the items returned, I had to check the condition of the items, process the customers deposit, the clean and shelve the items for the next rental. When tables and chairs needed to be delivered, I was the one who did that too. It was actually a pretty good job, but not enough salary to pay my newly acquired debt.

My night job at the 24 hour full service Scots Gas Station in near by Marlow Heights was a simple one. My main duty was to pump the 29.9 cent per gallon Sinclair gasoline, sell a quart of motor oil when asked, and to make sure the cash drawer balanced out at the end of the shift.

This two-job arrangement would have worked just fine, but this routine continued for a few weeks and was slowly wearing me down despite my youth. One night at the gas station it had been particularly slow, nobody had been in for gas since 3am and I was fighting to keep my eyes open. I lost the fight and at some point fell asleep. When I jolted awake I realized I had been out for fifteen minutes and still did not feel refreshed. Shortly my eyes started to droop again so I got up and locked the front door, turned off the switch for the gas pumps and put my head down on the desk for a few minutes.

My sleep was interrupted by the rude loud banging on the locked glass door by an irate customer wanting to purchase some of the 29.9 cent per gallon gasoline. After all this was a full service gas station, and he expected to have someone awake to perform this task for him- he had lofty expectations. Truth is I had been asleep for over an hour, with no idea how many customers had come and gone without getting any gas. I was fortunate that the man banging on the glass door wasn't my boss!

That evening I received a telephone call from the Union office directing me to report to a location in Washington, D.C. in the morning to walk a picket line in support of the strike. I protested to the official saying that I had a job I was expected to show up for in the morning. His response was short and sweet, he said there was not a choice if I wanted to continue in the elevator trade. My decision was made, I called Mr. Brinner at the rental store and asked for the day off for personal reasons. I told him that since I had not been upfront with him about the strike at the onset. I did feel remorse at not sharing with my temporary employers that I only needed work until the elevator strike was over. I was also aware that I would not have been hired in any capacity at either job, if I had disclosed that information.

His response was to show up for work in the morning or consider the job terminated. I walked the picket line the next two days.

A couple of days following my sleep attack night at the Scott's Gas Station I got a telephone call from the Marriott Restaurants General Manager asking me if I would be available to accept the position of assistant to the Chef. Without hesitation I accepted. With the rental store job gone, I could quit the gas station job and just work the higher paid restaurant position until the end of the elevator strike.

The very night prior to reporting to the Marriott Restaurant I received another telephone call from the same Union official, the Business Agent, Bob Templeton. Mr. Templeton announced that the strike had been settled and the strike was over. I was to report back to work the next morning. I was elated and relieved that I was getting my job and career back, but I was also dreading the telephone call that I must make to the General Manager of Marriott. I did call and I thanked him for his generous offer, but must decline after reconsidering. Honestly, I had been looking forward to the challenge of working under the Chef in a major restaurant chain. Who knows how that life path would have turned out?

BACK TO WORK

The following morning I reported to the Iverson Mall job site and worked there until the project was almost completed. Because I was the last helper hired and the elevator and escalator portion of the project was nearly finished, my employer Montgomery Elevator was reducing manpower, so I was laid off and sent to the Union Hall to seek another job with a different company. I was fortunate that another company had a need for a helper, so that same day I was sent to a company named General Elevator that had a production factory in Baltimore, Maryland, and maintenance offices in Baltimore and Washington D.C. The office manager for General Elevator introduced me to the mechanic I would be working with in the Service Department. As a team we would replace elevator hoist cables and swap out various defective large motors and generators. This service work was much different from the work I was doing on the installation of elevators and escalators.

Life seemed to be getting some sense to it, but there was still the Vietnam war. I was engaged to marry and I really wanted to have a clearer idea of where I was going and when! I tempted fate with the decision to quit Junior College and chose to volunteer for the Draft. This action would send my name to the top of the Draft Call list and put me in the military quickly. Going this route instead of enlisting into the service made my commitment two years in the Army rather than the three year tour enlisting required. Of course for me the advantages of volunteering for the Draft included allowing my military service commitment to be satisfied. By achieving that I would be able to plan on getting married, raise a family, and able to think about long range plans for my life. This wasn't possible with my military service still in front of me. I wasn't even able to choose a marriage date. Fulfilling my obligation I could go back to college on the G.I. Bill after I am discharged from the Army, and I would be resuming my career in the elevator trade. This decision was definitely the best I could have made at the time. It presented the best result possibilities for the different scenarios.

THE DRAFT

It only took three weeks until the Draft Board notified me requesting my presence in Upper Marlboro, Maryland. From there I would board a bus with other invitees to be taken to Fort Holabird in Baltimore, Maryland. We were told that we would get an induction physical before we could be accepted into the Army. That day I learned something. You would think that after years of gym classes seeing numerous naked bodies while we were getting dressed and showered would have erased all chances of embarrassment ages ago. The difference is that in gym class you knew everyone in the locker room. At the induction physical it was quite different! You are in a large hall with 300 plus naked strangers! We were directed to line up side by side five or six men deep, then told to bend over and touch your toes and stay that way. For most of us in that hall that day it was the first time anyone had ever grabbed our testicles and told us to cough. We continued standing in line getting probed and prodded. So much for any degree of modesty.

Among this varied group of young men there were almost as many different stories as to why they were there. You know my story, I chose to be there by volunteering for the Draft, but a majority of the guys were there because their Draft number had be drawn.

Some were volunteers for the three year tour program because they thought it to be a good job opportunity, and if it turned out after the three years they still thought the Army life was for them they could extend their service another three years. There were a few others that didn't want to be in the Army at all and were hoping to fail their medical exam. While there were still others that tried various tricks to try and skew the test results and fail the exam. One example of the later was a guy who rode on the bus with us. I overheard him telling his friend that he had applied a bar of soap to his underarms hoping to raise his blood pressure, I don't think it worked. After the Army was finished with us, we got back on the bus returning to Upper Marlboro.

Since I knew that any day soon I would be called to go into the Army, I was planning to quit my job at General Elevator. But was advised by my mechanic to work one more week as that would complete my six month probationary period and guarantee my employment and higher pay rate upon my return from the Army. That was sound advice that I always appreciated. I did work that additional week instead of taking a week mini vacation prior to leaving for the Army. After the work week was over I reported to the Draft Board in Upper Marlboro, Maryland to take another bus ride to Fort Holabird in Baltimore, Maryland – a one way trip this time. It was Army Induction Day!

Upon arrival we were herded into a large room with desks and administered a battery of tests to be used to determine what job in the Army we would be best suited to perform. The Sergeant who proctored the test advised us not to cheat by looking on other test papers since they are not the same tests, he said they used several different series of tests. He further advised us to do the best we could on the tests because you cannot fail them. There is a job in the Army for everyone, and the Army will find us a job! Being able to get out of the service at this point is almost impossible, but I remember one guy who rode with us to Baltimore that tried. Apparently he had been celebrating at his going away party the night before, and decided to continue his drinking on the bus to Fort Holabird. By the time we were testing he had already been loud and obnoxious toward the proctors. After warning him several times his conduct got worse instead of better. After the testing we were sworn into the Army and put in line to board the buses to Fort Bragg, North Carolina. But we noticed that our drunken inductee was being led in a different direction. He was escorted by a couple of "MP's", Military Police soldiers into a nearby room. We were told later that he would be charged with disorderly conduct and would be spending "bad time" in the stockade jail. It was called bad time since none of the time spent in the stockade counted toward your service time in the military. After he finished his jail time he would then start working on his two year commitment for the service. I am sure he didn't see that one coming. Bummer.

FORT BRAGG - BASIC

The long night bus trip to Fort Bragg, North Carolina was uneventful with most of us trying to sleep the entire trip. I suppose stress takes a lot out of a person and the mind and body needs to deal with it, our way of dealing with the stress at that time was sleep. Little did we know at that time what was in store for us upon arrival at the base the following morning. As the bus pulled up to our destination and slowly came to a stop, the driver opened the door and all hell broke out. The loudest, most demanding voice from the scariest uniformed man who came onto the bus screaming and yelling for us to get our sorry asses off the bus – and yelled we were already moving too slow. He continued yelling until the bus had emptied, which took less than three minutes, only to be greeted by two more of these yelling uniformed sergeants that put us into files and columns. We were terrified. No matter how tough we thought we were back home, we were out of our element – and into theirs.

The rest of the day was spent being processed into "This man's Army" getting issued boots, fatigue uniforms, socks, underwear, undershorts, wash cloth, towel, and a large cylindrical canvass bag to put everything in...everything olive drab green in color. Receiving our skinhead haircuts and getting immunizations with an air gun was special. A large portion of the day included being constantly reminded from the sergeants that greeted us that they were all important and all powerful, while we were nothing, worthless – we were dubbed turds.

We marched to our company area and were introduced to our new living quarters which was a single level World War II era building referred to as a barrack. We were assigned a bunk and an olive drab wooden floor locker. I got a top bunk, and when we went to bed that night it was to become one of the loneliest nights I have ever spent. Everyone feels lonely at times, perhaps really very lonely. But when you are missing everything you ever knew and used to being around, and you can feel the separation in the deepest part of your stomach and chest, and you can hear whimpering throughout the barrack in the still darkness – then you have not felt that degree of loneliness. Day one was over, only eight weeks to go!

After an extremely restless night of unquiet sleep, the following morning at five o'clock our alarm clock went off; except our clock was in the form of the screaming sergeant from the day before. Yesterday was not a dream! The sergeant worked his way up and down the rows of metal double – stacked bunks that ran from end to end of the previously condemned World War II building that had been placed back into service to provide the much needed housing for trainees. Another sign the Vietnam war was expanding. As he passed each bunk he would shake it violently to get the occupants out of the bunks and onto the floor. That was our first lesson in Boot Camp. We were taught that we were expected to move immediately when told to, and to move fast! Actually, the way that lesson was explained to us was him saying, "All I want to see is asses and elbows," which basically meant the same thing. We had to stand at attention in our undershorts next to our foot locker and wait for further instructions. Our instruction this morning were to get our shaves, showers, shits, be dressed including our undershirt, and be outside in the space between the adjoining barracks by five-thirty. Everyone scrambled as if a stink bomb had just gone off as we all made the attempt to be the first in the showers or grab a sink to shave and brush teeth. There wasn't even enough time to use the toilet for anything other than taking a quick pee. We all made it outside on time only to have the sergeant waiting to greet us with that now familiar demanding elevated voice. He grabbed our arms or shoulders, and pushed and pulled us into a pattern he had in mind arranging us side-by–side at arms length apart, four rows deep. He informed us we were now in "formation" and we were to assume that formation whenever we were told to "fall in." Our second lesson taught and learned. Now in formation, the sergeant led us through a series of exercises for the next twenty minutes – so much for the showers we took! After our exercises we marched in a gangly fashion to the Mess hall, which was the name for the dining room building where all meals were prepared and served. We went there at this time for breakfast, but each meal was referred to as "chow" and all of the meals were served by going through the chow line and having the food items spooned onto the plates. The same method the school cafeteria operated the lunch lines.

Breakfast is eaten all over the United States the same way, right? Wrong. I have lived in Philadelphia, Miami, and Washington, D.C. But what I was about to find out would prove to be an enjoyable experience. My Dad was in the Army during World War II and I often heard him refer to S.O.S. (Shit on a Shingle). Even at home Mom cooked this preparation using chipped dried salt beef that came sealed in a little glass juice glass and my whole family seemed to like it. But the Army had their own method of preparation, they used ground beef that was cooked in a thick white gravy and served over toast and it was up to us to smother that with Louisiana hot sauce found on every table – I loved it! Another breakfast item I was introduced to and found confusing was grits. I was filling my bowl with what I thought was Cream of Wheat, thinking it would give me a good start to the day. The guy next to me in line who was from South Carolina told me with a laugh it wasn't Cream of Wheat, it was grits. I thanked him and asked what they were used for and how do you eat them? He replied I was doing it correctly by having them in a bowl, but now I should add two sunny side runny-yolk eggs on top of the grits, then mix and eat. I loved that new discovery too!

After a not too leisurely breakfast, since everything is given a specified time to complete, and never at a leisurely pace, we marched back to our barrack area where we had a new surprise waiting; meeting our senior Drill Sergeant. We were ordered to "fall in" when a new sergeant appeared before us. In a very commanding voice he introduced himself as Drill Sergeant George W. Washington. He stated that "everything you do in Basic Training is a case of mind over matter. I don't mind and you don't matter." I am sure we all had the same thought after hearing that. We are done for it!

Drill Sergeant Washington was everything I expected to find in a professional soldier. From being named after our first president and carrying himself as a proud soldier, to the detail he gave his uniform. Sergeant Washington told us his ancestors were the original Americans, and you could see that in his Indian features giving him a very chiseled look. His rank was SFC-E7 grade, which is sergeant first class with 7 stripes. His uniform had razor sharp ironed creases and his brass belt buckle had a mirror shine to the highest luster. He wore Airborne jump boots instead of the issued type we all wore because he was also a paratrooper and was authorized to wear those type of boots. His paratrooper boots were also buffed to a mirror glaze. This whole look was topped off with the wide brimmed olive brown "Smokey the Bear" hat that only Drill Sergeants may wear. Quite an impressive figure of a professional soldier stood before us. All of us new turds were put off balance in the presence of this polished soldier that was very much in charge. Our new boss, Drill Sergeant Washington, launched into what was expected from each one of us as a soldier. He had only eight weeks in which to get us in shape and mold us into his and the Army's vision. What he did not disclose was the extreme rigorous schedule we would be keeping, and the many trials of endurance we would need to learn to overcome.

My dad gave me some sound advice before I had reported for duty, he told me not to volunteer for anything that sounded too good to be true, but be the first to volunteer if the chore did not sound desirable. This didn't make much sense to me at the time until I witnessed what he meant firsthand. The reasoning behind his advice was that Army personnel refer to every job and title in the context of an acronym or they give it an important sounding name. For example some nasty jobs are given an attractive name such as "DRO," which stands for Dining Room Orderly, a nice title that sounds pretty impressive, but actually meant you were a waiter that cleans tables in the Mess Hall. Another important sounding title was "Latrine Commander," a title that you would expect to wear the rank of officer on your uniform to go with the position. Actually the duty required the man with that title be responsible to clean the latrines, which were the bathrooms. "KP" was another trick title, it stood for "Kitchen Patrol" which sounded as if you were going on some sort of mission, but it was simply working in the Mess Hall kitchen.

Dad also told me if you get picked to work "KP" and you don't volunteer first to peel the potatoes, the alternate job was to clean out the nasty grease trap - not a fun task. As coincidence would happen, on the very first day in the Army the sergeant asked for a volunteer for "KP" at the Mess Hall, and I raised my hand. At that time I didn't know if I had volunteered for the best chore or the worst chore, as I was whisked right away to the Mess Hall. Arriving there I met the Mess Sergeant who seemed like a pretty friendly guy. He assigned me to the chore I had seen Beetle Bailey , a character in the comic strips, do for years, peeling potatoes. This was the job Beetle Bailey had to always do for punishment, and I volunteered for it. I always envisioned a twenty-foot-tall pile of potatoes that would take days to peel, one potato at a time, again I was wrong. There were a lot of potatoes that needed peeled, but now the Army had a machine that the sergeant called a growler. He showed me that when I put a bunch of potatoes into the hopper it would spin and grind off the skin. The potatoes didn't need to be peeled anymore- I actually felt disappointed. The rest of the night I performed various duties around the Mess Hall but nothing too taxing. After I finished my duties I headed back to my barrack to get some sleep before that alarm clock went off again at five. After that night I never had to pull "KP" ever again while in the Army. Thanks Dad!

"KP" was a job that most of the men tried to avoid at all costs, but yet when the Drill Sergeant told two of the turds they were going to a party they looked puzzled. The sergeant explained they were going to a "G.I." party that should last for hours. Turned out it was another name for cleaning the room from top to bottom, and the room he chose was the latrine. Got 'um again.

The following day Drill Sergeant Washington randomly chose one of the guys in our barrack to be the platoon guide. He was to be in charge of the group in formation now to be called the platoon. The platoon guide replicated real military structure because he was now responsible for all of the men in the platoon. He was the liaison between the men in the barrack and the Drill Sergeant. Unfortunately the person that was chosen as our platoon guide was not exactly suitable for the position. After he was chosen he was beside himself with pride and an over abundance of self importance. The pride was an understandable reaction, but it turned out he was rather full of himself also. Almost immediately he acted as if the rank of General had been bestowed upon him with stars on his shoulder, instead of the arm band bearing sergeant stripes that symbolized the platoon guide leadership position. Our appointed guide patterned his leadership style somewhere between a drill sergeant and Napoleon Bonaparte. He was yelling at everyone and commanding when it wasn't appropriate or necessary. His style was not effective and the men seemed to be turning against him. The guys did not like this chosen leader and it was becoming increasingly obvious to the drill sergeant that a change was necessary.

A change did happen. Apparently I was being observed helping a few of the men with their Drill and Ceremonies: The Army manual used for formations, marching, saluting and proper military etiquette. I had knowledge on the subject because I was in the Civil Air Patrol during high school. The Civil Air Patrol is an Air Force Auxiliary that I was a member of for a few years. We met on Andrews Air Force Base, did summer encampments at Fort Dix, New Jersey, and drill competitions at various bases in the Washington, D.C. Area. Drill and Ceremonies was identical for every branch of the service, and never varied. I never thought Civil Air Patrol training would have given me an edge years later in the Army. Drill Sergeant Washington dismissed the platoon leader he had chosen and gave me the position. Being familiar with Drill and Ceremonies gave me a jump start ahead of the other men in my platoon. My confidence was high, and after observing how the previous guide led, my style of leadership would be different. This leadership position felt right to me. Previously I made the decision to put every aspect of my life on hold until my military commitment was fulfilled. My goal was to perform the very best I could, make the most money I was able in the two years of military service, and to only serve my two years with no extended terms of service. Now that I was appointed to platoon guide the path was chosen, and I was beginning to realize my goal.

Performing my very best was determined by how I chose to lead, and my method of leadership was by example. By this I mean that if I was teaching someone how to do something such as climbing over a wall or crawling in the mud under barbed wire, I would be right there next to or in front of him performing the same task, even if I was excused from participating because of my position. Being platoon guide was more of a benefit for me than it was for the other men since it was necessary for me to be better than the others, and I attribute that necessity to the position. For example, in the hectic mornings when we were supposed to fall in and perform our exercises before going to breakfast, I was expected to be the first to be outside ready to go. Just as our Drill Sergeant had the spit and polish appearance that was better than his turds, my uniform had to be flawless, my brass buckle had to be able to see your face in it, and my boots needed to be spit shined and standing tall. When leading the platoon through the morning exercises, I had to perform better, despite the fact that there were several of the guys in much better physical condition than me. When we were running hard or marching for long distances I had to go faster and longer, and I could. It was a mind set of the position, not superior strength nor endurance. This was very good for me and the role I was in, and it was good for the others in the platoon because they accepted me as their leader, and I had gained their trust and respect.

Shortly after I became the platoon guide, one of the guys in the platoon came to me in the barrack before "lights out," which was the time all lights were turned off and we had to turn in for the night. He took me aside and asked me to do a huge favor for him. He was a married man with one young child and he missed them so much he was willing to do anything to get out of the Army and be able to go home and be with them. He was so desperate that he wanted me to tell Drill Sergeant Washington I caught him having sexual relations with another man. He was positive this shocking information would surely get him kicked out of the service. I tried to reason with him explaining that there was no good that would come out of this. I pleaded with him to reconsider since if the Army did believe him he would get a dishonorable discharge that would follow him throughout his lifetime. We went back and forth with the issue for twenty minutes or so with neither one of us gaining much ground. Finally with lights out announced I agreed to deliver his information in the morning. We then hit the bunks.

The next morning after exercises and Mess hall chow I found an opportunity to talk with the Drill Sergeant alone, but my presentation had changed.

Instead of telling the story the way he wanted it related, I told the Drill Sergeant the whole story, but not the soldiers name. I recounted how much he was hurting from missing his wife and child, and that from what I observed he was not gay. Besides there wasn't any other man he had sexual relations with, and in my opinion did not appear to be prone to suicide at this time. Sergeant Washington said he has seen men trying to get kicked out of the service many times in the past, and the usual reason turned out to be missing their sweethearts back home. But never using as drastic a tactic as this one. He told me to go back and tell the soldier that the Army needed the name of the man he had the sexual relations with. He was sure that a name would not be given since there was no other man, and there certainly would not be another man in the platoon that would volunteer to discredit himself in this way just to help someone else get discharged. Sergeant Washington advised me when I gave the man this information to try and convince him that in time he would tolerate being away from his wife and child. In time he would discover that he made the correct choice to remain. After I presented the response from the Drill Sergeant to the soldier, and worked hard trying to convince him to give it some more time, he finally agreed to stay and tough it out. For the rest of the time remaining in Basic Training nothing was ever said or referenced concerning that incident, and as far as I am aware it never went beyond the three of us to this day.

It was the end of 1967 and mostly everyone in our platoon either smoked or chewed tobacco, which reminds me of a story that every man in the platoon found funny, except for the individual it happened to. It was a typical day for our training and we had been on a long road march earlier in the day. When we arrived back to the barrack area the Drill Sergeant told us to "fall out," which you have figured out is the opposite of "fall in." He then yelled "light them if you have them," which gave us permission to smoke. After smoking his cigarette one of the guys just threw it to the ground and using his boot crushed it – Big mistake! One of the sergeants happened to be looking in his direction at that time and saw this infraction. We had been instructed when we were finished smoking our cigarettes to field strip them by tearing the paper wrapper and letting the tobacco that was left fall to the ground, then roll up the paper in a little ball and place it into your pocket. If a filter cigarette was smoked the filter was also tucked into your pocket to be disposed of later. The Drill Sergeant yelled for us to "fall in" then called the soldier up to the front of the platoon. He asked him if he knew what he had done, and from the look on his face he didn't have a clue and responded no. Then the Drill Sergeant informed the poor soul that he had desecrated his barrack area by tossing his cigarette onto the ground and grinding it into the dirt, it was now necessary to give that cigarette a proper burial.

I mentioned previously that our barracks were vintage World War II buildings that had been placed back into use for the Vietnam trainees. The buildings were about sixty feet long and twenty five feet wide, one level high, and built of wood. The building was built on piers of concrete block about three feet off the ground and was heated with an old original coal furnace that we had to keep stoked. The buildings had no insulation.

Back to the cigarette burial. The Drill Sergeant produced a newspaper and gave it to the soldier instructing him to retrieve the smashed cigarette and wrap it up with the newspaper. After the soldier accomplished this he was instructed to climb under the barrack until he reached the center of the building and bury the cigarette in the newspaper. He was instructed to dig a hole three foot deep using only his bare hands. Fortunate for the soldier that the ground was sandy soil and not hard earth, but a three foot hole is a formidable task, especially when you don't know what else is under the building with you. While he was digging the rest of the platoon were told to line up side-by-side in order to "police" the entire company area. When one man screws up, we all pay for the mistake. Now the company area encompassed our barrack and three others, and "police" entailed picking up every bit of thrash that was directly in front of our walking position. This also meant anything that was not to have grown in that area needed to be picked up. Everything we did was training. The reason we were being punished for something we didn't do was the military training way. All members of the platoon are treated as one unit. That is the basis of team building. So because one man messed up, we all did, and we all suffered. Most of our punishment for most all infractions was push ups. The sergeants would tell us to assume the front leaning rest position, and they would bark out how many push ups we had to do. Usually given in multiples of twenty or more depending on how bad we messed up. It seems we always had a man on the ground doing push ups. When we made our way through the company area with our pockets full of various pieces of unauthorized ground debris, we were put back into formation to witness our "gravedigger" emerge from under the barrack. He stood up with his uniform all dusty and sandy and presented himself at attention to the Drill Sergeant. Sergeant Washington asked him if he buried the cigarette, and he said he did. He asked him how deep the hole was, and the soldier said proudly, three feet deep. The Sergeant Washington asked him what was the headline on the front page of the newspaper. Oh No! I can't even describe the look on the soldiers face! His expression had gone from a satisfied smirk to an instant blank unbelieving stare. The Drill Sergeant made him crawl back under the barrack, dig up the newspaper, read the headlines, and bury the package again. I think he was under there a little too much time to accomplish that task. Maybe he was doing additional reading just in case there were more questions when he came out. This was just one of the methods of training used during those times. Nobody liked it, everyone agreed it was harassment, and nobody could understand what lessons we could possibly learn from this. But somehow we were learning, and we were remembering what we learned – amazing!

Another memorable moment occurred on a Sunday afternoon. Sergeant Washington showed up at the barrack on his day off wearing his civilian clothes. I never thought there was a chance he wore anything other than military issued uniforms, but to be honest he still looked as if he was in a uniform of sorts. With him was his twelve year old son. He gathered us all around the pull-up bar and lifted his son to the bar. The boy quickly knocked out thirty pull-ups then dropped to the ground with a smile from ear to ear on his face. Sergeant Washington announced that even a twelve boy was able to do more pull-ups than most of us soldiers. It wasn't a surprise that the boy showed us up, as we were used to being outdone on a daily basis, Sergeant Washington routinely could do more push-ups and pull-ups, run longer and faster, and hold a rifle in an extended position longer than any of us. And this was not just an observance I had made, we were reminded often. Again, bringing his son in on his day off was not meant to put us down, rather it was a continuance of our training. The purpose was to urge us to raise the bar and step up our efforts to excel. His method was effective.

Basic training was intense, as it should have been. The

training was geared to each of us becoming an infantry rifleman no matter what MOS we were to be assigned at the conclusion of the eight-week training, considering we passed the final physical performance testing. The battery of tests taken back at the induction station at Fort Holabird determined what MOS (Military Occupational Specialty Code) you would be assigned. For example the infantry rifleman is designated an 11B-10, and the Army has close to two hundred of these MOS's.

One of our platoon members was having a particularly difficult time performing the various physical goals we had to reach in order to pass our eight-week training cycle, and not be recycled as a result of failure and repeat the eight weeks again. Recycled men would drop back to a platoon in training behind us, which meant you wouldn't know anyone, and everyone you had been with for eight weeks had proceeded to the next training location. No one wanted this. The problem he was having stemmed from his excessive weight. His civilian job was in a bank and it was apparent that in his life before the Army he did all of the wrong things. He overate, ate the wrong things, and of course was too sedate never exercising. The first seven weeks of our training schedule was to drill, march, exercise, qualify at weapons ranges, and attend many classes on various military subjects. The eighth and final week of our training was concentrated on practicing our skills to pass the final physical performance course test. This preparation was in addition to our regular training schedule. The last week was the most intense because to be able to graduate out of Basic, everyone had to meet or beat the standard times and repetitions that the Army determined was necessary to pass. For instance, every man had to be able to do a certain number of pull-ups, and a certain number of push-ups, beat the minimum time to complete the obstacle course, or hang and travel rung-to-rung on the parallel bars in order to get to the determined needed number to pass. That was a major challenge our overweight buddy had to overcome since as I mentioned the punishment for failure was to be recycled. Failing set you back to repeat the entire eight weeks again and retake the physical tests. If a soldier failed another time he would be recycled yet again. We had a man in our platoon that was on his third recycle, but it wasn't going to happen again because our platoon had become a team and we all determined that nobody would fail the test.

The team spirit was the driver for the overweight banker to push himself further than he had ever gone before. He was pushing so hard he was bursting blisters he had built up on those soft hands of his, and at times he pushed himself so hard he would break down and cry. But with the help of the entire platoon he was getting through it. On the day of testing we were all in much better condition than when we had stepped off that bus eight weeks earlier, including our banker. As we all went through the circuit of physical test feats, anyone that saw our banker falling short of achieving his necessary test score would jump to his assistance. Several of us that had already completed the circuit went back to his position and cheered him on and sometimes ran beside him to keep him going. The result was that everyone had passed the tests, and because our banker passed with our help the team effort made us all winners. Everyone would advance to the next stage of training, after the

Pass and Review Parade for graduation was completed of course.

The following day we found ourselves back in the building where we had initially received and signed for our olive drab clothing issue. But this time we were being issued our Class A dress uniforms complete with shirt, tie, socks, dress black shoes, and a rimmed cap. The class A dress uniform was a dark green uniform, that I would have my private first class stripes sewn on when I got home. We were finally going to look like the soldiers in photos we had always seen. The Army wanted us to look good because each of us represented that branch of service. Tomorrow we were expected to march in perfect formation in a several company sized graduation parade in front of the "Brass," which was what we called the top ranking officers of Fort Bragg. In the grandstands we paraded by were also many invited officials and guests and other observers, two of which were my Mom and fiancee. The end of a cycle of training parade was a pretty big deal for the military community, and it was especially special for us. With all of the pomp and circumstances, just for us "turds," how could our chests not swell with pride. When the ceremony was completed we went to the headquarters building and received our orders for our next duty station. The men we had been training with would now get orders for their particular MOS's and scatter across the country to the respective advanced training base locations, I would never see many of the men ever again. After we had our orders we got into the line to process off the base, and collected our pay. At that time we were released to go home until we had to report to our next duty station. That information was on our orders. I met up with my Mom and fiancee and drove back to Maryland.

Prior to leaving home for Basic training my fiancee and I made the decision to get married when I came home after that phase of training was completed. Between her family and mine they would handle all of the many details planning a marriage entails. They arranged for the wedding service to be held in my neighborhood church named Holy Family, and the reception would be in the church hall downstairs under the church. Both families prepared food and supplied the beverages for the event. Tuxedos were not needed because my Army uniform served as my wedding outfit, and as luck would have it, my buddies John and Mark were home on leave during this same time so they wore their dress uniforms also. My good friend Paul was there to complete my side of the wedding party. We all had a good time eating, drinking and dancing. After the wedding reception, my new brother-in-law Gene gave us his apartment as his wedding gift to us to us, to use for our honeymoon. Time passed quickly, and before long it would be time to go to Fort Polk, Louisiana for "AIT," Advanced Infantry Training for another eight weeks of training.

Before the wedding ceremony there wasn't too much time to make the rounds and visit with family and friends, but I needed to make time to meet with my best friend from school, Johnny. He had gone through the same Basic training at the same time as I did, only his was in Louisiana. We got together and swapped notes and stories of our past eight weeks of training, and what the following eight weeks of training might bring. I only had a total of nine days before I had to report to Fort

Polk, Louisiana, not an abundance of time to relax and regroup, but I made the most of it spending as much time as possible with my new wife, family and friends. When the time came for me to leave and head to the airport, the good bye scene was just as bad if not worse than leaving for basic training. I wonder if the visit and down time is really worth the grief of saying good bye again? I don't know.

FORT POLK – AIT

My orders had me going to Fort Polk, Louisiana to spend another eight weeks in "AIT," which stands for Advanced Infantry Training. Yes, just as I thought I was chosen to be a ground soldier in the Infantry and my MOS would be that 11B-10 designation. This was not a surprise for me since I volunteered for the Draft. Despite qualifying for other MOS's in the vast availability the Army has, those jobs were held for the men that volunteered for three years or more as enticement to join. Makes sense to me, why go into the field to fight when for an extra year or two you could get a job as a clerk behind the front line at headquarters. Many volunteers even stayed stateside and never had to go to Vietnam. I knew I would be assigned to Infantry, and I was alright with that, since it was my choice to serve two years and be done, but I still wasn't 100% sure what being infantry meant – I would find out.

Travel to Fort Polk was interesting, aside from the fact this was the first time I had been on a plane larger than a J-3 piper cub type plane that I had helped to rebuild for a project with the Civil Air Patrol. My itinerary took me from Baltimore Washington Airport to Atlanta, Georgia, and at Atlanta I caught a plane to New Orleans. From New Orleans I took another flight on an airline named Trans Texas Airlines, that the locals fondly renamed "Tree Top Airlines." TTA's fleet of aircraft were old even for those days. The plane I boarded had two wheels in the front under the wings, and a smaller set of wheels that it rested on back at the tail section. I remember seeing this type of aircraft in the old Humphrey

Bogart movies, maybe Casablanca. The passenger list for this flight was filled with soldiers in uniform, and only a few civilians, so everyone was going to Fort Polk. Shortly after take off an elderly flight stewardess, (she had to be at least forty years old. I was only eighteen and my perception could have been skewed) went to a red ice chest cooler embossed with Coca Cola on its side, located behind the seat next to the only exit door on the plane. She removed three six ounce bottles of Coca Cola and proceeded to pour the contents of those small bottles into yet smaller three ounce paper cups. With her tray of miniature beverages in hand she began her beverage service rounds for the passengers. Somewhat of a different experience we had on the TWA (Trans World Airways) flight we had just been on earlier. Anyway, that was the start of the no frills welcome we were getting already, and we were still one hundred miles from Fort Polk.

Upon arrival we were met with the buses that would deliver us to the base. Our clothes, and all of the rest of our worldly belongings were packed into a canvas duffel bag. This awkward piece of "luggage" was fitted with a strap that would sling over the shoulder and because of its shape, size and weight would have to be carried in a less than military stature. With duffel bag in tow we got off the bus and presented our orders to the sergeant that was there to greet us. Not much was said to us at that time, which was fine for me since I was tired and dragging from the flights from Baltimore, Atlanta, New Orleans, and Fort Polk. Fort Polk was just outside a small military town called Leesville located in the Northwest sector of Louisiana near the Texas border. Upon arrival to the Headquarters complex we disembarked our bus and were told by the sergeant that rode the bus with us to fall into formation.

After we were in formation the sergeant had us form a single line in order to enter the building in front of us to begin yet another processing. Yes, it seems a pattern is becoming evident to me. We will need to go through the drill of processing at every new base we report to from now on. By this time we had a handle on what was expected of us, and we already had most of the equipment that we needed, except for the M-16 rifle we were assigned to be our responsibility for the next eight weeks. At this point I had not fired the M-16 since it had just been designed and designated as the new military issue personal weapon for American soldiers. The previous rifle that was the standard issue was the M-14 rifle that dated all the way back to World War II and used in the Korean War. We qualified on the shooting range with the M-14 in basic training, and all of our Drill and Ceremonies training was with that rifle. The M-14 was a heavier conventional weapon that was very accurate. It weighed nine pounds empty and almost eleven pounds with a loaded clip, and when fired you definitely felt the impact on your shoulder. On the other hand the M-16 rifle was lighter weighing around six pounds empty and seven and a half pounds with a full clip. It was shorter in length and had the ability to fire at a faster rate with just a flick of the selector switch which had three settings: Safe, Semiautomatic, and "Rock and Roll" or fully automatic. The rifle sights used for aiming at the target were mounted on top of the barrel and was also the carrying handle for the rifle. The only flaw we noticed, and was constantly preached to us, was that if not kept impeccably clean, the rifle might misfire. The other minor trouble was that it was not conducive for Drill and Ceremonies activities due to the sight handle configuration and the sleekness and length of the rifle compared to the M-14. Both of these problems seemed minor in the scheme of things since we were required to keep our weapons clean at all times anyway. The lightness of the weapon would be a plus for those extra long road marches we had been promised.

After our processing was completed we were marched back to the bus and taken to the other side of the base to our new barrack. I say new because I never saw it before. It actually looked very similar to the Fort Bragg barrack. We would find out later that they were the same World War II vintage that had also been pressed back into service for the Vietnam War escalation. The buildings had been declared unfit to live in, but that pertained to their structure only. The insides of the buildings had been used by trainees for years and therefore had been cleaned, waxed, and shined daily since they started to be used back in the 1940's, and will now continue in 1968. The reason I even mentioned the age of the buildings at Fort Bragg and now here at Fort Polk was that the non insulated wooden structures with the original plumbing in the latrines (bathrooms), and the coal furnace heating, the buildings were considered fire traps. Luckily no issues ever occurred while I was in either location due to age or condition of the barrack.

When we got off the bus this time there were two more sergeants waiting for us. As the doors to the bus opened they started the familiar yelling we had gotten used to. But this time they didn't call us "Turds," our new name was "Shit birds." They screamed orders for us to get off the bus and into formation, but there was a difference this time. When the same scenario happened in Basic Training the sergeants were terrifying and believable and it was all new to us. This time even though we still hustled to get off the bus, the yelling sergeants appeared to be trying too hard to be fearsome. Maybe by this time we were getting used to this type of fear- method training, or maybe the trainers in Basic just had the advantage of surprise for the new troops. Either way, I wasn't as impressed with them as I was with the model of a soldier I saw in Drill Sergeant George W. Washington.

We were assigned bunks and given our orientation class from the Company Commander while we were in company formation, he was the first officer we encountered directly since joining the Army. He outlined the next eight weeks of Advanced Infantry training we would be receiving, and the importance it meant for each of us and our fellow soldiers to learn the skills the Army was about to teach us. Learn the skills in order to fulfill our goals and help us to return from Vietnam alive. The Captain informed us our training was the best in the world, and our mission was to crush the Vietcong. This was a new term we learned to call our enemy. The entire orientation was meant to get us pumped up, and it did. Our training company was comprised of four companies and was nicknamed the Tiger Battalion. Everywhere we went in our battalion area was reference to the Tiger, and every minute we were awake there was someone doing something to keep our fighting spirits high and alive.

Competition was always in the forefront of our daily lives. We were competing between other companies, between platoons within our company, between Squads within the platoon, and between individuals. Our fighting spirits grew as our eight-week cycle progressed, and our knowledge and acceptance of being a fighting soldier was growing as we learned about explosives, shooting and qualifying with new weapons. We also attended range classes where our support weapon groups demonstrated their fire power using the big guns like the 105 Howitzer. It wasn't all field work we were involved in, we also took classes that reminded me somewhat of High School. The classes were held in auditoriums, and the instructors were professionals with real teaching skills. Their MOS's were not 11B-10's. The subjects that were taught were much different than the English and Math classes we had all taken. These were geared toward what we would use in military life.

The typical classroom session was on a particular weapon such as the M60 machine gun, teaching us rate of fire, weight, and type of ammunition it used. We would be divided into small groups and be brought to tables with M60's on them. We would be taught how to disassemble and then assemble the guns multiple times until ingrained in our minds. We then would be packed into long open semitrailer trucks and taken to the firing range to continue our class by learning how to properly fire the weapon. After a few hours of practice and burning through thousands of rounds of ammunition, our skill was tested on the targets for qualification. We had to have a certain number of hits in the target circles at a certain distance to determine the award badge we would be awarded and wear on our dress uniforms. The rifleman badge was the lowest qualification and since every man had to qualify, this was the badge most awarded. The sharpshooter badge was the next level of marksmanship, and the expert badge was the highest awarded. I was fortunate enough to qualify expert on every weapon ever fired in the Army, although I did have to qualify twice to be upgraded to expert from sharp-shooter on one weapon.

Other classes we took would not be typical of those found in High School or College. For example the Booby-trap and Explosives class. The classes were of course held outside with three sets of bleachers that were packed with the entire Company. We were in the sun and it was another hot day, and together with the lack of sleep that we all shared, you could see the toll it was taking on the troops. The instructor was in the midst of showing how the Claymore Mine functioned and the proper and safe way to set it up having the firing side pointed toward the enemy or else you could blow yourself up by mistake. All of a sudden, without any warning a large explosion went off under the center set of bleachers. Well, needless to say, the entire company came alive, especially the multi-tude of those that had been dozing off to sleep. No one left the bleachers since it wasn't possible to move the way we were packed into the bleachers cheek-to-cheek. But before chaos could break out the instructor had us all sitting back down - calm but shook up. The instructor explained that "Charlie," another name for our enemy, would try and surprise us the very same way. We will have to learn to always stay alert and aware when we were out in the "Boonies," which was any area that was not secure in Vietnam. He said "Charlie" would booby-trap or rig explosives to anything that might cause harm to us, his enemy. We were advised "learn to avoid the temptation to kick a can on the ground or step on a paper bag, it could contain a bomb and be the last time you ever kick."

Another range class we had was for the Hand Grenade. Again we first had a class demonstrating different types of grenades from other countries. Then the separate components of the grenade were displayed, and we were taught why it was able to have a kill radius of five meters, and how to treat and handle the grenade safely. Following the formal class we proceeded to the hand grenade course which was constructed of many, many sand bags (I wonder who filled those.) There was a pit with sandbags around the front and sides. Inside an instructor and a trainee were standing facing the front of the pit. The trainee was handed a live grenade from the instructor, and at that time the trainee was supposed to wait for the command from the instructor to pull the pin. Then hopefully immediately throw the grenade forward at least seventy-five feet, and then duck behind the sandbags for protection from shrapnel.

In addition to the outdoor Range classes and exercises, there were the field operations performed during the daytime and or at night. The majority of the training instructions were during daylight. Subjects on how to read and properly use a compass was an important class, but before we were even ready to learn the compass we were required to find our one hundred meter measure. Every individual has a particular number of steps it takes to walk a measured one hundred meter course.

This is because of leg length, walking style, and gait. It sounds easy, but in order for each individual to walk the course and come up with the same number of steps each time was difficult. Every soldier had to walk at the same stride while counting his steps on the course until the count was the same each time when reaching the end of the course. This was a necessity since when you are told to leave one location and proceed to another location, and the only address you have are coordinates on a map, you depend on a compass and your individual one hundred meter count. The compass lets you determine the direction, and your numbered steps measures the distance you have traveled to that location. The reason the step number was so important was that in case the terrain was thick and impenetrable, and impossible to walk a straight line at your measured stride. A couple of soldiers could use their step numbers and that would insure a better average between them to get a good distance measurement.

Army Rangers had a method to keep track of how many one hundred meter segments they had traveled. They carried a string with knots like a rosary, when their pace count reached one hundred they would advance a knot on the string. This helped them keep track of the distance. Our instructor said that when we got to Vietnam and find ourselves in the "boonies" we would find the terrain varies from a rice paddy to thick lush tropical jungle, to a large stand of bamboo that can't be penetrated without machetes. Keeping track of your steps was harder because you sometimes had to go around areas and try not to get lost. This lesson came in handy especially at night. Another good tip he gave us was that after taking your compass reading, look straight out in front of you for a hundred meters and pick out a landmark. A distinctive tree or small hill would be a good choice. Head to that reference point, and when you reach that reference point repeat by picking another reference point each subsequent time until your destination is reached.

Finding your way through the night is only one of the challenges encountered. Safety is also imperative. When we were in training we used blank ammunition for our rifles in our field exercises. We were to assume it was live ammo, and being safe was not aiming or firing our weapons in a direction that would possibly hit another soldier. I know this sounds like common sense, but in the pitch black woods at night, when there are instructors dressed in black silk pajamas just like "Charlie," the Vietcong, trying to shoot you, mistakes can happen, and do. We were on a night field operation and were given the objective to go from point A to point B within a certain length of time and that the out of bounds or restricted areas would be indicated by white construction tape. There was a half moon and clear skies, so after we got away from artificial lighting our night vision improved. After about fifteen minutes we were able to see shapes and contrasts clearly. We traversed the course reading the maps, watching our compass, counting our steps for distance, and waiting for a hidden instructor to jump out and "Kill" or capture us. We were at a heightened state of awareness, and that is when the unexpected happened. There was a group of six of us walking two abreast when all of a sudden we were startled by something directly in front of us on the path. Right before we got to them and nearly stepping on them, several large unknown animals ran in all different directions away from us, thankfully no bites were received. But it scared the shit out of us all. It wasn't until we finished our field operation that night and were telling our animal encounter story, that we found out the animals were armadillos, a prehistoric looking animal that was about the size of a raccoon. But when we saw them in the dark, the armadillos seemed the size of wild boars. I never saw things like that back home in my neighborhood. Yes, there are many challenges in the night field operations, and we were still in the friendly States.

Nearing the end of our "AIT" Advanced Infantry Training we had to go through the combat obstacle course. The course was divided into two sections. One was a daylight road march that ended at a strength/ability course which consisted of wall climbing, rope climbing, and rope swinging. We also had to run through water and mud obstacles, and walk across logs in water trying to maintain our balance. The second course was at night where we had to crawl with our rifles under strands of barbed wire through dirt and mud puddles a distance of twenty-five meters while live fire with tracer rounds from M60 machine guns were fired over the barbed wire. While we were crawling explosive charges were being set off all around us. Needless to say, it seemed very real and it was. If for any reason we popped up before reaching the end of the course, it would be our end. The ammo was live!

Nearing conclusion of our required training, an offer came down through the ranks to us that a brand new program was being started. It provided for additional training in Infantry skills that could advance our rank to the grade of E-5 Sergeant waving the time usually needed for time in service to achieve that rank. To reach that rank it would normally take nine to ten years in the service, and even then, it is not an automatic promotion. To be eligible for the program, the Company Commander needed to choose four soldiers out of the entire AIT graduation class cycle, and after that each individual that was chosen would have to volunteer for the program. Afterward the paperwork would be sent up through Headquarters and eventually our orders would be changed. So since I was destined to go to Vietnam following AIT, the new orders would have me reporting to Fort Benning Infantry School to attend this new program instead.

I remembered what Dad had said about volunteering, but this was different. This fit into my initial goal of doing the very best I could and to achieve the highest rank (for the additional higher pay), for the two years I was going to serve in the Army. If I was asked to join the program I would do it, I would take the opportunity, even though it felt strange to make such a gigantic decision that would surly take my life in yet another direction without guiding advise from my parents or a counselor. The first opportunity I had to direct my life direction was enrolling in college. The second was volunteering for the Draft. Big decision to make, but in my mind pretty straightforward: serve two years, get out, get married, live life. This next opportunity was much larger in scope than the others. Taking this path would give the Army the okay to invest even many thousands of dollars more for my training. Money spent to mold and shape me into a combat leader, a professional fighting soldier.

This decision would change the direction of my life in the military, and none of my family or friends knew anything about it.

The Commanding officer chose the four soldiers and fortunately I was one of them. I was pleased with myself that I had volunteered, and beyond pleased that I had been chosen for the program. I felt special. We still had to continue with the AIT training cycle, but I was already looking forward to my next adventure.

The final days of training were comprised of preparing for the Pass and Review Parade which signaled completion, and of course processing out of the training cycle. This time during processing we were given an Army green dress uniform and brimmed hat. Since everyone that finished AIT in good standing was awarded the rank of "PFC" Private First Class, we could wear that stripe on each arm sleeve of our uniform, but we had to have it sewed on ourselves. I was awarded a good conduct medal that would be worn on the uniform as well. In all fairness, this medal was awarded to everyone that was able to stay out of the stockade. Other items worn on the uniform were the Infantry Blue lanyard worn on the right shoulder, and the blue backings for the brass emblems, and weapon qualification badge awards worn on the pocket. The uniforms had to be ready to wear by parade day. When the uniform came back from the tailor with the unit patch and private strips sewn on, I polished my brass using a product called Brasso. It had been used since World War II, and maybe before then. Once all of the brass was polished, I put the Infantry Blue backings behind the brass infantry crossed rifles insignia. I installed the blue Infantry rope under the right collar tab, and spit shined my new black dress shoes. When the whole outfit was together it looked good, really good. I wouldn't be surprised at all if there were some soldiers that enlisted just to wear the dress uniform. In fact I know that for the Marines that had to be a certainty. The Marine Corps has a drop dead good looking uniform; it has to be a major draw to get additional enlistees.

The Pass and Review Parade was even larger than the parade we had at the end of Basic training. The spectators attending the parade ranged from parents and wives seeing their loved ones prior to them shipping out overseas, the top ranking officers of the post, to local followers that just like seeing a good parade and marching band. The parade was quite a production of pomp and circumstance with the Flags, a Battalion of soldiers in their brand new decorated Dress uniforms, all marching in step and perfectly lined up side to side and front to back, with a marching band playing familiar patriotic tunes we all knew, and that snap of the heads when passing the grandstand, with Platoon leaders presenting the crisp hand salutes all at the same time. It was pure entertainment. The formations were very impressive to watch, and most impressive to be part of.

For my graduation and Parade in Basic Training my fiance drove my Mother down to Fort Bragg, North Carolina for the festivities, and I was very happy to see them after eight long and hard weeks of training. The parade for AIT was a different story. Graduates for this training had to travel from all parts of the United States to get to the Base that specialized in the MOS classification they were assigned. Many times it was too far for family and friends to make the long drive or suffer the expense and time to fly. The spectators we had for our Pass and Review consisted of the residents of the area close to Fort Polk, or wives living on Base or on an overseas assignment. After the ceremony was completed we went directly to Headquarters and processed out and collected our pay. With that completed we were free to leave for home.

Everyone that day scattered in different directions using many modes of transportation. I had a bus ticket to New Orleans, Louisiana for a flight I was going to take late that night. Unfortunately the bus ride for the two hundred miles to new Orleans was a local and taking forever. I had been on the bus four hours and we had only gone twenty miles away from Leesville, which was just outside of Fort Polk. I could have waked faster than that. And that is how the rest of the trip went. We stopped at what seemed like every stop sign to take on a new passenger. I felt anxious the entire bus trip with my airline ticket in my pocket that was getting worthless as the time was eaten up minute-by-minute. We arrived hours past my flight departure time. I missed my plane and now would have to fly standby.

Flying standby wasn't bad because if there was room on a flight it was free or very cheap to the military. A nice benefit for a low paid soldier. The problem was that being so close to Fort Polk with the graduation of a big class just taking place, most of the flights were full. Which meant I would be spending the night in the New Orleans airport. My overnight at the airport wasn't the most comfortable. I was able to find a couple of empty chairs at a boarding gate. I made the attempt to get comfortable by putting my stuffed duffel bag in the chair beside me and that gave me something to lean against for support. I was so tired I don't remember when I fell asleep, but I did and was able to grab much needed shut eye. My sleep was an on and off again restless sleep, due to the airport traffic and noise. Thankfully the following morning I was able to pick up a flight and was heading home.

All of the attention I received after finally arriving at the house was a little overwhelming at first, but did ease after awhile. I was a little embarrassed about being the center of attention, but in another way I liked being welcomed home. Everyone was glad to have me home and I was very glad to be home. After sixteen weeks of intensive training I was full of new knowledge, and I was in the best physical condition in my life. I was also bursting with pride for what I had accomplished in training and what I was about to go through in the coming months with Fort Benning Infantry School. My beaming pride was obvious to others too, I think because of the way I was carrying myself now. I had a total of fifteen days of leave and after the bus ride fiasco in New Orleans was now down to fourteen. I had two priorities while on leave. First I wanted to visit with all of my friends and family, and second I wanted to party late into the night with my buddies. The problem accomplishing both was that I felt sleep deprived from waking up super early during the past sixteen weeks, and it was great not having anyone yelling for me to wake up and hit the deck. So I took advantage and slept in most mornings.

It was over too soon. My leisurely life style had come to an end and I had to say good byes and head to Georgia for the next phase of my life.

FORT BENNING – INFANTRY SCHOOL

The Infantry School located at Fort Benning was a military college that previously allowed only men learning to become officers from the "OCS" Officers Candidate School, or officers that would take courses of study in order to advance in rank. Invited distinguished foreign ally military officers would also attend the school and take specialized classes, and would then return to their countries to teach the information to their troops. Now for the very first time the individuals chosen to be the first in the Army's pilot Sergeants program would be attending this prestigious institution, the finest military college in the world, and I was one of them!

Our program consisted of nine weeks of Infantry School formal classroom studies, and range classes. Among the subjects at the School were tactical mathematics, military theory and tactics, extensive emergency field medical training, and numerous other subjects. The next three weeks of our training was based on Ranger Training. Rangers are an elite branch of the Infantry, along with the Special Forces, known as the Green Berets. Both units take extensive training that is similar to each other, but the Green Berets spend more time training in the medical arena, and the rangers spend more time on tactical and combative training. The Rangers wear a red beret as part of their uniform. Membership in both of these units are only available to the most dedicated and the best of the best.

Processing completed, (yes more processing) we were taken to our two level concrete block building barrack. Inside we were assigned a bunk, footlocker, wardrobe locker and a desk. Big change from my previous lodgings.

The drill sergeants had us fall into formation. They then laid out most of the main requirements and rules we would need to adhere to for the next twelve weeks. The sergeants informed us that we were now on a merit and demerit system, and that the score at the end of the program would determine if we passed or failed the program. If we passed the program the number of merits would determine if we were advanced to the rank of E-5 Sergeant. One outstanding individual in the Company could be awarded the rank of E-6 for academic excellence. Another individual could be awarded the rank of E-6 for excellence in performance and skills as a leader. The rank of E-6 awarded through the normal process in the Army is usually attained after being in the service approximately fifteen years, and that is not automatic either. The criteria was to excel scholastically and exhibit strong leadership qualities. That was the golden ring hanging out there for us, and it was quite a prize within our reach. The size of this first class numbered approximately three hundred, and all were chosen to be the best of the trainees in AIT, and they all wanted the elevated rank. This was not going to be easy.

There wasn't any hesitation getting our program started. The Drill Sergeant pulled a surprise barrack inspection while we were at morning Mess (breakfast). When we returned to the barrack we found bunk mattresses thrown to the floor at several locations, footlockers upset and tossed onto other bunks, desk drawers open, and so on. In civilian life you would swear a break-in occurred. Practically everyone got "gigs" or demerits for a wide variety of infractions. A few of the infractions were for not having our bunk sheets tight enough, and if the sheets were tight enough, the covers were found to be too loose. If there wasn't the correct fold on the mattress sheet corner we got a gig. The footlockers had been tossed because they either contained the wrong piece of clothing, or the correct piece of clothing was improperly folded. If everything in the footlocker was not in its proper place as dictated in a template we were given the first day, we got gigs. We were all upset and angry for the way the inspection was conducted, with us absent and behind our backs. On top of that we felt our personal property was violated. One of the guys had two photographs of his wife posing in the nude (meant for his eyes only,) thrown on the bunk. The quick accumulation of gigs, or demerits resulting from that surprise inspection so early in the program angered us also. From this time forward we would now be taking a defensive stance with regard to our sergeants.

The fact is that the shock effect at the beginning of this program was exactly what the Drill Sergeants and top brass planners of the program wanted to accomplish. The Army was not about to spend tens of thousands of dollars on each of us, and award us with higher pay from a grade increase to the rank of E-5, without testing our every fiber of character makeup. The program is meant to take us out of our comfort zone and push us past our limits at every turn. The rewards were too great and the responsibilities we would be given were too immense to expect an easy ride or being able to coast through this program. In theory every soldier in this pilot program could train the entire twelve weeks and finish the program and not be awarded the Sergeant E-5 promotion. The criteria is the soldier excel and stand out as a leader before being promoted. So if every man was loaded down with demerits nobody gets promoted, and we all continue on as PFC's. The Drill Sergeants wanted to have each of us looking and acting the same as everyone else in the program, to conform to each other and to promote competition among ourselves. Inflicting gigs or demerits was their way of control over us. A few of us had already figured this out, the Army wasn't about to pull something like this on the first class in a Pilot program that was probably sanctioned by the Pentagon and Congress. There will be promotions where deserved, but it's going to be a long twelve weeks.

Every class we attended at the Infantry School had its own textbook, and the textbooks had a certain location and order when on our desks, as well as a certain number of pens and pencils, the proper number of sheets of paper, certain number of folders, and even the paper clips, all to be placed in a predetermined location on our desk. We all conformed not to get the demerits.

When we were in Basic and AIT, our instructors would train us by showing us objects blowing up. Now we are learning how to wire the devices to blow up the explosives, and then we were the ones blowing up the objects. One of the classes taught us how to use C4 (Composition C4) which is a malleable plastic explosive that we could shape into any configuration to direct the blast exactly where we needed it. An example would be to roll the C4 into a rope the size of a pencils diameter, place it along the spot on a tree where you would normally use a chainsaw to cut it down. Next attach a blasting cap and spark igniter to the C4, and take cover. When the C4 ignites the tree is blown clean at that spot without blowing the tree apart in a million pieces.

Another class taught us how to neutralize many types of mines by disarming them. Land mines mines and booby traps, both US and Vietnamese types, were prevalent throughout the war zone and had to be dealt with daily.

We had grenade training in AIT, but the Infantry School took the instructions a step further. We learned about all types of grenades, including the smoke grenades. For the smoke grenades they taught us why, when, and how to use them. The instructors taught us what the different colors meant, and what the enemy knew about our smoke signal meanings. We learned by observation what a White Phosphorus grenade was, and how it was able to be placed on top of a truck engine block or any metal surface, including a tank and burn all the way through to the ground and still be burning. Tremendous heat in one grenade the size of a peanut butter jar.

Our range training on the weapons we were already familiar with and had qualified with went much further than we had previously learned. We were introduced to a few more weapons that we had to qualify on the range such as the M-2, 50 caliber machine gun. We had a range class teaching us about the gun and then we got to fire a few of the gigantic rounds at the range. Enjoyed that class. What an awesome weapon.

The M-79 grenade launcher was a short gun that looked like a sawed off shotgun with a three inch shaped barrel approximately eighteen inches long. To load it a latch was flipped to the side allowing the barrel to break open at the breach. A large fat round of ammunition over two inches in diameter and six inches in length would be placed into the barrel end closest to the stock. It then would be snapped close as with a shotgun. There was a multitude of ammunition rounds available for this weapon which made it very versatile. The High Energy (HE) round was the most used since it replicated the hand thrown grenade. The HE round could easily be shot a distance of seventy-five meters with accuracy, and still have a kill range of five meters. Another round that was used mostly by the soldiers walking point in the thick jungle, was the shotgun round that contained hundreds of needles or pins that would spread out in a wide pattern in front of you when shot. This round was used in case you encountered something or someone in front of you by surprise and the distance was too close to aim. It was meant to take out anything in your path that you could see.

The M-79 even had a "Willie Peter" round, which was a white phosphorous round that sent out small pieces of that burning agent seventy-five feet in a wide pattern upon impact. There was a noticeable indicator that you had been on the M-79 firing range. When the weapon was held and fired improperly, by griping the gun and wrapping the thumb over the top of the breach as you normally do with all other rifles, the M-79 would kick when fired. The latch that opened the gun would cut the hollow between the thumb and forefinger. Since this was a very painful mistake it usually happened to a person only once. Effective learning lesson. Since the M-79 was introduced it changed the structure of the platoon. Now there were two men designated M-79 grenadiers, carrying the M-79 instead of an M-16 rifle like most of the other soldiers. Along with the M-79, he humped many different rounds of ammunition and usually had others carrying a few additional rounds for him to use.

The next weapon we qualified with classes and demonstrations was the Army's pistol, the 45 caliber hand gun. This was the Army's standard pistol since before World War II, and is truly an amazingly powerful armament. Our classes taught us about the moving pieces of the gun, how fast the rate of fire, the distance it could be fired accurately, and how to load and shoot the pistol. Other classes showed us how to "field strip," disassemble the weapon into its smallest component parts, and then reassemble it. Performing this exercise was done so many times by us that we could do it blindfolded by feel alone. To pass that class we were timed on how long it took to disassemble and reassemble the pistol. We also had a demonstration to observe the effects of a 45 caliber round penetrating different objects. This was meant to show what would happen to a man hit with the round. First it was shot into a paper target, and it acted as any other pistol or rifle rounds; it just went through it producing a hole. The instructor fired it into a gallon jug of water next. There was an explosion of the jug as though it was hit with a ten pound hammer. There was a huge impact and damage to the water jug was total.

The other special weapon we had classes on was the M-60 Machine Gun, by far one of my favorite weapons. The M-60 weighed twenty-three pounds and fired the NATO round, a 7.62 X 51 mm bottle necked rifle cartridge developed in the 1950's. And also fired tracer and armor piercing rounds. It was the same round that fit the

M-14 rifle used in basic training. It was called the NATO round because our allies around the world in the NATO Alliance Partnership all used the same size ammunition. Our classes on the M-60 were similar as the other classes. We learned how to assemble and disassemble the machine gun in order to clean and lubricate it. This was imperative due to the enormous number of rounds that this weapon fires in such a short time period. It must be kept clean and lubricated to prevent jamming and therefore taking this firepower out of commission in combat. When we got to the firing range to live fire the M-60 we separated into two man teams, one man was the shooter and the other man handled the ammunition feeding into the gun. The belts of ammunition had to be clean and fed into the gun straight and steady to prevent jamming. After one man had his turn shooting he would switch positions with the Ammunition handler to allow him to become the shooter. During my session with the M-60 the range instructor spent more time at my location on the line than anywhere else on the firing line. He kept offering me extra instruction and tips on the weapon which allowed me to spend more time on the line. Afterward he asked me to be his demonstrator shooter for the class in the bleachers.

The three sets of bleachers were again packed for the demonstration class, maybe they need a fourth set. I was on the firing line as the shooter with another soldier representing the ammunition handler, and we both had yellow helmet liners on just for the demonstration. The instructor was standing in front of the bleachers with microphone in hand. He instructed me to fire two long bursts on the machine gun, with which I complied by firing two, twelve to fifteen rounds immediately with just a touch of the pulled trigger. The instructor told the class that the long bursts just heard represented the normal operation of the M-60. The next command I was given was to fire two short bursts, which meant firing three rounds twice, which I did. The instructor then told the troops in the bleachers that the three-round burst was meant to replicate an automatic rifle firing, instead of being identified as a machine gun. He continued saying that the enemy would be more interested in destroying the man with the machine gun because of its superior firing power. Of course this same rationale applied to US soldiers also. We were taught that the textbook structure in the platoon was to have two M-60 machine gunners and two ammunition bearers. When the instructor completed the explanation he turned again to to the firing line where I was still lying behind the M-60. He commanded me to fire three, one-round shots, and I did. In order to be able to do this, the lightest of touches and quick release on the trigger was necessary. I was able to accomplish this as ordered thanks to the extra attention and tips the range instructor had given me. The instructor once again turned back to face the bleachers and said the lesson to be learned for being able to fire one round at a time was two-fold. First was that it could be done. The second was that if you ever found it necessary, you would be able to disguise yourself as a regular rifleman instead of machine gunner, or if you were running low on ammunition and needed to conserve.

In order to graduate from this phase of the program we had to pass the Ranger Confidence Course. This course had two separate obstacles.

In order to pass the Ranger Program the trainees in that program had to complete the Ranger Confidence Course also, but they usually went through the first course one day and then went through the second confidence course a week later. And they certainly did not go to the course directly from taking a twelve mile forced march with rifle, loaded ammunition belt, and full backpack. Since the Army's top officers were monitoring our program with much scrutiny, it was decided that this pilot class would run the Gauntlet different than the Rangers did, to show that we were possibly tougher and to justify the programs existence. Therefore after having just returned from three nights on field exercises, and humping everything we had with us for twelve miles we were now going to run both obstacles in the Ranger Confidence Course the same day, one after the other.

At the conclusion of our twelve mile forced march we ended at the Confidence Course, stacked our rifles, removed our ammo belts, and dropped our backpacks. We were divided into two groups, half would go to each obstacle test. The line I got in was named the telephone poles. It consisted of a ladder twenty-five feet tall and attached to the first telephone pole. After climbing the ladder and reaching the top there was a platform to stand on that was four-foot square that faced the water over a pond. Another two poles were placed in line continuing over the water twelve feet apart, each having two 2X12's nailed to the tops of the poles. At the end of the further pole out over the water there was a 1-inch diameter rope about Fifty feet in length strung out over the water and facing the bleachers on land. The Ranger instructor in charge was decent enough to have one of his men demonstrate how the obstacle was to be performed correctly. His man climbed the ladder to the platform, then waked, almost ran, across the 2X12 inch boards the entire twenty-four feet out across the water. Reaching the end of the boards he reached down to grab the rope that was attached to the pole. He swung himself under the rope until his arms were extended while holding onto the rope with his hands. He was now facing the shore as he moved along the rope until he reached about twenty-five feet. While facing the Ranger Instructor in front of the bleachers he requested permission to drop into the water. When given permission, he dropped and swam to shore. The permission time to drop into the water varied in time. Sometimes the instructor just had us hang there for awhile just to see how long we would hang on before dropping. Watching the demonstrator run across the planks made us think this wasn't going to be too difficult, after all, if he could do it, then we would. But we found out that it was because after that first demonstrator ran the course, the poles were shaking and really swaying. He ran it when everything was still, we were set up. When it was our turn, we had some of the men in our group refuse to try and do it at all, some men tried who couldn't finish, and then others who just sat down on the boards and scooted their way to the end where the rope was. I did the course but did not like it. I had the fear that if I were to lose my balance and fall, the results would be fatal. After I finished swimming to the shore, I got out of the water and ran, as we were told to do, to the other obstacle test.

This test we were calling the cable test. I climbed a forty-foot long metal ladder that was in an open pipe tube enclosure; probably enclosed to prevent a tired soldier from falling back and falling. Upon reaching the top there was a small platform facing out over the pond, with an instructor to greet me. Two feet above my head was a ¾ inch cable stretching from where I was standing over a hundred yards over the water. This cable ran with the shore where there was another set of bleachers and Ranger instructor standing in front. On the platform the instructor would put a trolly device onto the cable with a bar on each side for our handhold. When he was ready, I was told to pull myself up to the trolly on the cable. When I did that I took off down the cable. On the way down the cable, the instructor at the bleachers would give us the command to let go and drop. The distance he gave that command varied, and nobody ever got close to the end where the distance to the water was less. If the soldier did not drop when the instructor told him, he had to repeat the test until he did. This being such an important high profile program for the Army, the bleachers at each obstacle were filled with the Army's top Brass and many invited guests and observers from the Infantry College and other officials and officers from our Allied countries.

Pleased that the tests were finished. We all felt very accomplished making it through the three night encampment, the twelve mile march, and completing both confidence courses. We would find out later that the classes that were to follow us would not take the Ranger Confidence Course as we did, instead it would be divided to be taken a week apart the same as the Ranger program was structured.

During our twelve weeks of training we were told there would not be any leave or passes until after the third week of training. This seemed like a long time before a break, but that was how the program was structured. The way it turned out was that when the three weeks were completed, the sergeants found a way to deny us any time off. Those merits and demerits mentioned earlier could be given away freely at the whim of the sergeants; some fairly given and some not. One example of a fairly given demerit was on surprise inspection, when the sergeants entered the barrack and shouted "fall in next to your bunks." Everyone except for a man on the second floor was standing beside his bunk at attention. The reason for this was when the sergeants went upstairs they found that soldiers entire bunk was missing. It had been taken downstairs and set up outside as a prank, and unfortunately the sergeant found the bed missing at the same time the soldier did. We all had a good laugh, but it cost us. This was fair, but many other times very minor infractions such as a pencil out of place, or a pair of underwear wasn't rolled into a tight enough bundle, or numerous other minor infractions were cited and awarded demerits. Nobody ever saw a merit given. Such a strange system. It was our consensus that this was a "Chicken Shit" method to evaluate us. We would have preferred to be rated on our actual merits and performance.

We were heading into our eighth week without having been on leave when something that would change our country happened; Martin Luther King had been killed. Around our country, especially on the East Coast major disruptions were taking place. Riots, fires, looting, and all types of property destruction were scarring our country, and tearing it apart. We were the closest military base to Atlanta, Georgia, and we were put on high alert to be called into action for riot control if needed. The next day mandatory riot control classes and live practice was started. This was in addition to our regularly scheduled training. This was a new and unwanted expectation. Yesterday we were training to go overseas and fight the Vietnamese enemy. Today we are training to fight against our fellow Americans in our own country. Will we be able to do this? Thankfully we were never called to respond, the National Guard from the various states and the various State police forces were called for crowd control. We continued our training.

Not being granted leave until our tenth week brought the men in our barrack closer together as a team unit, especially on the first floor where I lived. The sergeants told us that after Friday's training we would be given overnight passes but would be restricted to a fifty mile radius from the base. My fellow team members all agreed that the overnight pass was too little too late and was a joke! A fifty mile radius wouldn't even allow us to go to Atlanta. We made our plans. As soon as Friday's training concluded, everyone piled into cars and taxi cabs and headed to the airport. Having money from not being able to get a pass before, we now bought airline tickets. I bought my ticket to Baltimore to go home just for the weekend (stretching the overnight pass). As bold an action as this sounds, I was nervous as hell doing this, but it didn't seem wrong. It felt like we deserved it since when we leave Fort Benning after graduation, we have to report to our next assignment for another eight weeks without getting a break to go home. Our training day wouldn't start again until 5 am Monday morning, and I made it back by 11 pm Sunday night. I thought I was safe. Walking around the barrack checking on the others, I found that most of the guys on the first floor, and a few on the second floor also flew home. My flight was only a short hop to Baltimore, but some went to New York, Florida, and Connecticut. One man even went to Minnesota (he wasn't back yet). My comrades proved they had balls that weekend. The following hours were like watching a marathon race waiting for the last runners to drag in. By 5 am Monday morning every last man had made it back and was ready for the day's training, all with better attitudes. Funny thing though, we could have easily kept this major infraction to ourselves- but we didn't. Someone pinned their canceled airline ticket to the bulletin board, and within five minutes everyone else had their tickets there also.

Well, after the sergeants discovered that display they went wild. They threatened to toss us all out of the program, they exercised us hard trying to run us into the ground, and they marched us until we ran out of time for the next scheduled class. But that was it. After all, what were they going to do? Go to the company commander and tell him seventy percent of the platoon went "AWOL," (Absent Without Leave.) Absolutely Not! The inquires that action would raise for this pilot program that was already being watched so closely, would cause such a stink, and bring havoc down on the platoon sergeants and company commander. Someone always has to take the blame. Nothing further happened on this matter, and training continued for the next two weeks.

At the end of the twelve weeks those men who were to graduate were awarded the stripes for Sergeant E-5. We walked across the auditorium stage to receive our promotion certificates, as we saluted the presenting officer. A scholastic award for academic excellence was awarded to one individual (as per the program guidelines,) and he received his promotion to Sergeant E-6, Staff Sergeant.

After the ceremony, we went through our "Processing out" of Fort Benning. We were paid and received our orders for our next assignment. We actually knew we were returning to Fort Polk, Louisiana, and this time it would be different. We would be the platoon sergeants. I headed to the airport for the trip directly to Louisiana. No home visit this time.

For those of us that passed and received our promotions to E-5 viewed the programs fast-track sergeant creation terrific. But I noticed from the very beginning of the program there had been a jealous attitude among the seasoned sergeants who had come up through the ranks the hard way- the normal way. Some got over it in time and moved on, but some others kept that hard edge against us, and would rather see us fail in our training. We fail-the program fails. At first we were oblivious to this, but as time went by we encountered individuals that did not try to disguise their feelings. Those of us in the program with the newly awarded E-5 stripes on our sleeves were referred to as "Instant NCO's." "NCO" means Non Commissioned Officer, which is what all sergeants from the rank of E-5 through E-9 were. When we arrived to our company Headquarters at Fort Polk we were greeted by the First Sergeant E-8. He was a very seasoned sergeant with many years in the service, and was one that did not agree with the program. He let us know it. We were shown to our barrack and told we would be meeting the Company Commander at a later date.

The new E-5 sergeant I was to share my room with was named Johnathan Black, he wanted to be called by his middle name Joe. Joe was married and his home was Tampa, Florida. Our room was located on one end of the barrack, and the latrine was located across the aisle from our room. Not a big room, but our bunks were not stacked, and we each had a locker, as well as a foot locker. Rank has it's privileges, a phrase I had heard many times. Since we were here only three months or so ago as trainees in "AIT," Advanced Infantry Training, we remembered what we were supposed to do. Simply do what our sergeants had done with us. So at five in the morning we would be out in the bunk area shaking the bunks and yelling to get the troops out of their bunks and onto the floor. After that we would stay after them to hurry getting latrine duties completed, getting dressed, and getting outside for morning exercises before being allowed to go to Mess. I again took charge of the morning exercises, and I added a short run to the Mess Hall. We had a seasoned sergeant assigned to each platoon who presented our schedule for training each day. We would then carry out those scheduled duties.

It was the new E-5's duty to teach the trainees in their platoon everything they needed to learn in their AIT cycle. There was only eight weeks to mold these men into fighting machines. The better we did to train them, the better chance of them coming back from Vietnam alive. And there was also the chance that some of these trainees might be serving under us in Vietnam, and the better skill level they achieve, the better our chances were of returning to the States alive. We therefore showed real interest in their training, and at the same time built upon our leadership skills. I continued my style of leadership I had used since Basic training, only to find that the Infantry School leadership method was the same - lead by example. After all the School's motto was "Follow Me."

Our daily routines ended in the evening with the "Lights Out" command for the barrack. At that time every man was expected to be in his bunk for the night. The exception was for our room that still had the lights on for an additional hour, which for us meant an hour less sleep. The extra time was used to get our uniforms ready with ironed creases for the following day. We had to buff all of our brass to the highest shine, and spit shine our boots to a mirror finish that had to outshine every troop in the barrack. A little secret revealed. While we were in Fort Benning, the home of the Airborne Paratroopers, I learned that they kept their boots looking like patent leather by applying a thin film of GloCoat, a commercial floor tile polish, after spit shining their boots. No one ever knew how we always had the best shines, even the other new E-5"s.

We also kept our hair cut weekly. My roommate Johnathan, who went by Joe, asked if I would give him razor cuts, which was shaving a line pattern on his forehead and around to each ear and around his neck. This razor cut bypassed his normal hair line and established a hairline that didn't have any indentations. I gave him a razor cut weekly. We became good friends, and when we got a liberty pass to leave the base we took a taxi cab to the closest town which was Leesville, Louisiana, referred to "Sleaseville". A name it truly deserved. The town was a poster child for what a military town stood for. Business owners and others worked hard to cater to the base personal, and help them donate their money to the town. There was a house of prostitution that everyone in town knew about and the police did not bother to interfere with this business. We did not make any purchases there, but instead visited the testosterone filled bar. It wasn't too long before the first fight broke out, and we headed back to the base, stopping in the NCO club for a few drinks in a quiet setting.

One of our classes was Rappelling. Rappelling was wearing a harness to support your body while descending down a wall or out of a helicopter on a rope in a controlled manner. The class took a couple of days to complete, but we didn't mind because it was challenging as well as fun. We learned how to create a rappel seat made of rope and knotted in several places to form a harness. We learned where to put the D clips, and how to position our hands while rappelling down the wall. The important part of the lesson was learning control. The rope ran the height of the fifty-foot tower, the D clip would hook onto the rope, the right hand (brake hand) would take the rope and hold it behind in the small of the back. The left hand grabbed the rope on the other side of the D clip facing the ground. The idea was too descend the wall in short jumps of five or six feet at a time until landing on the ground. We climbed the stairs on the back side of the fifty foot tower to a platform that could hold several men. On the platform was a Rappel Master that monitored us to see if our equipment had been assembled correctly and was safe. On the ground there was another instructor standing a pace or two from the wall holding the rope that was affixed to the top of the tower, he was a "Belayer," and he was to break the fall of the man rappelling in case he was falling. To start the rappelling the man at the bottom of the tower would yell "On Belay," hearing this, the man on top of the tower would back off the platform and put his feet on the wall that ran the entire length of the tower. No movement was possible until the man would take a little slack in the rope and push off the wall. That would drop him down the wall two feet or more at a time until he reached the ground. At that time the Belayer would yell "Off Belay," which cleared the next man in line to descend the tower. Our Rappel Master had his arm in a cast from, you guessed it - rappelling. He said he wasn't injured by the method being taught, there is another rappelling style. It is called Inverted Rappelling. He told us when you are at the top on the platform, you can pull a third of the rope onto the platform, instead of the normal foot of rope, face away from the wall looking straight to the ground, point your leading arm and holding the rope. You then aim toward the ground and dive, never touching the wall on the way down. The rope we were using had a stretching value of a third of its length, so if you pulled up a third, and it stretched a third, you would free fall for almost twenty feet before the slack would catch and you were on the ground. His arm was broken because he miscalculated the slack. He said we weren't allowed to try the Inverted

Rappelling in the formal class, but since we had some time off the following day, a couple of us could return and try it. Myself and two others returned in the morning and he was there. What a wild experience that was, free falling looking directly into the ground as we fell, until the jerk I felt when the slack gave out, and then reversing my position and landing on my feet. The three of us made several rappels, and yes we kept experimenting pulling more and more rope up on the platform, until we found the rope calculation that when the slack gave out we were at the ground on our feet.

The training cycle was going well, classes in the auditorium, classes out on the ranges, drilling and marching, all was progressing nicely. I watched the trainees mature into fighting soldiers men, and it felt rewarding that I had a hand in making that happen. I found it difficult not get a full nights sleep due to the schedule I chose to follow. I would stay up later than everyone else preparing my uniform for the following day. I was driven to outshine every trainee as well as all of the new sergeants. I also made it a point to be up and dressed before anyone else in the platoon. I felt the impact of less sleep as the days went on, especially in the classroom situations. So while the class was in session I would always be on my feet walking the perimeter of the auditorium checking for trainees and some of the new sergeants taking a nap. The trainees got irritated with me trying to keep them awake, the sergeants were grateful. Keeping everyone awake kept everyone out of trouble and avoiding disciplinary actions, which usually resulted in dropping to the ground and doing many repetitions of pushups. It wasn't until after the fourth week that we had a Company Commander meeting for all of the sergeants, new and seasoned. He held the meeting at Company Headquarters in his office that was of decent size to accommodate us all. But it did get very warm with all of us in there. I took a seat on the leather couch in the back of his office. His rank was Captain, and as he stood up behind his desk with a cigar in hand, he told us how he thought the training was progressing. His observance was that it was good, but wanted us to push the trainees harder since the company was competing against the other companies in the Battalion. The judging of the competition would be at the Pass and Review Parade at graduation. On top of that, all of the new E-5 Sergeants were also being judged to see if one sergeant from the Battalion would be promoted to Sergeant E-6. The Captain must have continued talking, but I didn't hear anything because I passed out. The soft comfortable leather couch, the very warm room, and my accumulated lack of sleep finally did me in. I don't think I was asleep long, but that didn't matter. The Captain looked in my direction and saw my eyes closed. He got so raving mad that anyone would have the nerve to fall asleep while he was talking, as if I had planned the whole thing. Since this happened in front of the other sergeants I'm sure he felt he had to make an example, he told me to get out and report to Battalion Headquarters. I knew where Battalion Headquarters was and I went there.

Upon arrival I told the First Sergeant I was told to report, and what had happened. He told me to take a seat. I sat there for two or three hours before the Captain came through the door. I was anticipating being thrown out of the program. I had already been thrown out of the company. Instead the captain said that he was allowing me to return to the company to finish the cycle. I was very surprised with this news. I was positive I was gone, and I was feeling pretty low. He continued saying that the reason he was taking me back was because all of the new sergeants as well as the seasoned sergeants came to him and rallied to my side in support. He had been told how I was spending more time awake daily in preparation for the next training day, and during those training classes how I was keeping everyone alert and awake, including them. He went on awhile longer, but in the end I was allowed to return to the platoon. Back at the barrack I thanked my fellow sergeants very much for lending their support for me. I continued my training with the realization that any chance of getting promoted to the E-6 was far gone. I vowed to continue to lead as if I would be rewarded for my efforts. I did this for me.

When the trainees were going through their confidence course test I crawled on my belly in the dirt and mud with them, crawling under the barbed wire urging them by yelling to crawl faster and push harder. I wasn't expected to go through the course with them, I was allowed to stand off to the side with the other sergeants and wait until the trainees finished. But it seemed right to me that I should be crawling in the slop right next to them.

One area of training that I took charge of was Drilling and Marching. Both of these activities gave me and the men a lot of satisfaction. The drilling I taught them was called "Monkey Drill" which was a showy type of Drill not found in any Army manuals. I learned this style of drilling when I was in the Civil Air Patrol. It was a snappy, exaggerated form of drill that sounded and looked good. The men really liked to show off in front of the other platoons, who would at times just stop and watch us. Sometimes we would be doing our proper by the book drilling, when I would call out a command and change to "Monkey Drill" style moves. When we marched, and we marched everywhere we went, I led the formation by calling out military cadence. Which was meant to keep everyone in formation in the same step. It simply was calling out "Left, Right, Left," at times while marching. Well that gets boring quickly, and it sounds like all of the other platoons marching, so I started using marching phrases I had heard at Fort Benning. I would shout out a phrase or lyric and the troops would sing or yell back a response that would replicate what I had belted out. This kept the men in step as well, but it also kept the men pumped up since when they marched they sounded loud and proud, and looked great. One of marching phrases went like this, I would shout out something, then while in step the formation would shout it back. Such as, "Sound Off, 1,2, Sound Off, 3,4 Sound Off 1,2,3,4." Or "Here we go, To Vietnam, All the way, We are ready." Or "Everybody knows, Wherever we go, Who we are, We are the First, The mighty mighty First." And one more, "Ain't no use in going home, Jody's got your girl alone, Sound off." Whenever we marched anywhere we were always noticed, heads would always turn because we sounded and looked good, and we did it with conviction. The morale of our platoon was high, and it showed in performance.

It was around that time period Sergeant Black started calling me Sergeant Fury, the Army hero character in the comic book series. He said he called me that because I seemed to be everywhere doing everything in such a "Gung-Ho" style. I thought it funny at the time, but others started to refer to me by that name also, and the name stuck. Times like when we were at the Grenade course reinforced the nickname. I was stationed inside the sandbagged pit. The soldier would enter the pit facing me. I would ask if he was ready and he would answer. Then I would tell him to take the grenade from me, pull the pin, and throw the grenade at least seventy-five feet down range. Then most importantly duck behind the sandbagged wall. So I handed him the grenade, he pulled the pin dropping the grenade onto the ground, and then panicked. I knocked him back on his ass, reached down and was able to get the grenade and throw it down range about thirty-five feet, then grabbed him and pulled us both down behind the sandbagged wall. Wow, I almost didn't even have to go to Vietnam to get killed.

The last week of the trainees cycle was occupied with preparation for passing the final obstacle course events and the Pass and Review Parade. But Battalion called an assembly for all of the leadership cadre, including everyone from the new E-5's to the Battalion Commander who was a Colonel.

The assembly was to let us know that we did a great job, and to announce if a new sergeant would be promoted to a Sergeant E-6. After a few officers stood and gave a speech they called out my name to come forward. The Colonel then said a few words that I can't even remember, because I was in a state of shock and disbelief, and then awarded me the promotion to Staff Sergeant

E-6. What an unreal series of events and circumstances that had brought me here.

When we marched in the parade we were in perfect formation standing tall and looking good, and our Company Commander did win the battalion award for our performance. We processed out again, getting paid and receiving our orders for the next duty station-Vietnam. We headed to the airport to go home for our leave, but this time a few of us shared a ride instead of riding the bus and losing a day of leave again.

When I got home I had a couple of weeks before I was to go to Oakland, California to take a flight to Vietnam, and I tried my best to make the most of my time. The time flew by too quickly and when it was time to head to the Baltimore Airport, I left with my best buddy Johnny who was heading on the same flight to Chicago and then on to a different destination for more training before going to Vietnam. His longtime girlfriend Judy, and my new wife drove us to the airport. We had lunch together at the airport and then had our emotional goodbyes that needed to last us a whole year. Johnny and I flew to Chicago and we were both glad we had that opportunity. We were able to have our deep conversation like we used to do back home. Upon landing we separated because we were heading to different departure points. Johnny was going to be a helicopter pilot with the rank of Warrant Officer, which is the equivalent of a E-9 or E-10 pay grade. It was necessary for him to stop at Fort Hood for some additional training before he shipped to Vietnam. It was a year before I found out he had been assigned to the 101st Airborne Division, known as the "Screaming Eagles" and that he was not allowed to become a helicopter pilot because his eyesight was not strong enough to pass the eye test. He wanted to be a pilot; it was his life's passion, but he had to settle for helicopter crew chief, and filled in as a door gunner on helicopters.

At the conclusion of my Infantry School training at Fort Bragg I asked to sign up for the three week Airborne Training which was also at Fort Benning. I was denied the request because I needed to have one full year in Vietnam, and if I was allowed to take Jump School, I would be two weeks short of that year. Now the reason I wanted to go to Airborne Jump training wasn't because I was thrilled about jumping out of a plane, it was because qualified Airborne received extra pay called jump pay. I found out that the only way to continue to receive the jump pay was to qualify every three months and make three jumps that day. With that new information, and learning that there were no longer parachute jumps in Vietnam, I was fine not being allowed to go. Turns out I would only collect the extra pay for the first three months, and I would be out of the service before I could make another jump. It wasn't worth it just to wear the "Airborne Badge" or "Wings" on my uniform.

The comment of parachute jumps no longer being performed in Vietnam was due to an incident years prior. In the early days of the Vietnam conflict the 101st Airborne Division planned to drop a very large contingent of troops into a drop zone near Hue, Vietnam. Usually the advantage of sending paratroopers into an area is the element of surprise, but not in this case. The word got out that a large operation was planned using paratroopers. All the enemy had to do was find a huge clearing away from trees that would accommodate a massive parachute jump. There was only one place in that area that would handle the jump. The battle that ensued was horrific, the 101st was ambushed and shot at while they were floating down, before they reached the ground. That was the last jump in the 'Nam.

I flew a commercial airline from Chicago to Oakland. When I arrived at the Oakland Processing center there was a check-in that gave me a flight assignment to Vietnam, it was for the following day. A group of us that had just checked in were taken to a building full of bunks with just mattresses - no bedding, and a latrine. We were told to find an empty bunk and check the bulletin board for our departure time. Thinking we would have hours before any posting would occur, a few of us went to the closest bar. That was the first time I tried the Coors beer I had heard so much about, and it was good. Bottled in a short bottle it was a full-bodied beer. Had a couple of beers then headed back. Well, when I got to Oakland the temperature was in the eighties, but when the sun went down the temperature began to go down too. It dropped into the sixties at night, and that felt cold since we didn't have bedding to cover up with. In the morning chill we got herded to Mess, and by the time we finished eating the temperature was already climbing- Thank You! My name popped up on the bulletin board, and I went to the location indicated, got checked in and hopped on the bus to the airport to board a Trans World Airways flight. Except for the way we were dressed, this almost felt like a vacation flight. All of the stewardess were overly friendly and treated us great. Then it hit me; they knew where we were heading, and knew some wouldn't be flying back. Anyway, that was the reality. Our flight took us to Hawaii to offload a few passengers stationed there, and pick up a few more going on to Okinawa. There we offloaded more passengers and fueled the plane. We took off on our last leg of the trip our final destination. So far the flight has taken twenty-three hours and we were about to land at Tan Son Nhut Air Base, Vietnam.

ARRIVING IN COUNTRY

When we were on our landing approach to Tan Son Nhut, we didn't know what to expect. Were we going to be bombed or shot at by the enemy, if so, where would we go? What would we do? As it turned out we just landed without any problems, and disembarked the plane into a humid ninety degree, dusty, clay, non-green environment. Not what I expected. The evening news back home was always referring to this place as "the jungles of Vietnam. " Activity was everywhere I looked. Nobody just stood around. We were gathered up and taken to another holding barrack to wait and see where we were to go. Our names were called out letting us know which units we were to be assigned. Mine was called and I was on the way to the First Division "The Big Red One." I was on the way to Battalion Headquarters in Di An, pronounced "Zian," which was located outside Saigon in southern Vietnam. When I arrived with a couple of other assignees we were greeted by a tall Big Red One monument that stood about fifteen or twenty feet tall and looked just like the red number one on the division patch. I was pleased to have been assigned to the First Division because it was one of the units I was a little familiar with, and it was "First." As time went by I was able to learn the rich history of the Division. In World War I, World War II, and Vietnam history was made. From the beach landings in Anzio, Italy in World War II, to being the first unit to land in Vietnam, the Big Red One continues to bolster it's name and reputation everywhere it serves.

We entered the building to begin the processing

into the First Division, received additional apparel such as jungle fatigues, green fiber and black leather jungle boots, a camouflage nylon lightweight cover, and some new underwear. We was assigned to our platoons and told where to report. Mine was Company C, 1st Battalion, 2nd Infantry, 1st Infantry Division. Myself and three other men were taken by jeep to the Lai Khe base camp to join our units. We were dropped at a building that was used for the company headquarters, and that is where we met the First Sergeant. Not being a bashful type he told me right away that he did not believe in the program that gave me stripes after only one year in service, and I was going to have a terribly hard time "in country" because of it. He further said that due to a low soldier availability resulting from a high number of casualties, I would be the new 1st Platoon Leader, instead of a Platoon Sergeant like the textbooks read. The platoon sizes were now down to thirty-five instead of the forty-five men strength they are meant to be. The platoon leader would normally be a 1st or 2nd Lieutenant, but they also weren't available, so as a Staff Sergeant E-6 I was the ranking man. Damn, third day in country and I was given the responsibility of an entire platoon, and to change the dynamics further, my platoon sergeant was a "Buck Sergeant," E-5 and had thirteen years in service, and ten months in country. I was off and running from the very start.

The first Sergeant gave me directions to my assigned "Hootch" or barrack, which was a building with wood halfway up the walls and screening continuing to the roof. The roof was made of galvanized tin, and filled sandbags were around the outside perimeter all of the way up to where the screening began. Inside was a line of bunks on each side, each having a footlocker that had a combo lock on many of them. Since my platoon was in the field on maneuvers, I had to wait for their return. That night was spent in the hootch with only three other men, and there wasn't much sleep that night due to all of the new sounds we heard. The B-52 Strata Fortress Bombers dropped "Big Bertha's" which were five-hundred pound bombs, all night. Not that I knew what the explosions were that were heard, or how far away they were, or even if they were caused by us, or the enemy. The following day the company returned, and the men looked ragged. After they had a chance to get cleaned up, store their gear, and finish lunch at the Mess Hall, I was introduced as the 1st Platoon leader. I was greeted by indifference and an air of bother, another (FNG), F**king New Guy. Not exactly a warm welcome.

For the next couple of days I didn't try and offer any guidelines, rules, or advice. I needed to learn their way, not teach them mine. I tried to listen more than talk, and started the task of learning about the men I was to lead, starting with my Platoon Sergeant. He was "Boonies" smart from already being in country for ten months, and could teach me a lot, if he would. Not too thrilled at having to serve under a Sergeant E-6 that had only one year in service, and zero experience in the field, the platoon sergeant had plenty of reason to wish I just never happened. It did take time for him to accept me, then respect me, and then to follow me.

It was obvious to me that I needed to get up to speed quickly and to find a way to gain the confidence of the men, so I decided to go out on "LP's" which were Listening Posts. The LP's were comprised of three men that would go out and position themselves about three-hundred or so meters outside the perimeter of the main body of troops. The purpose was to be the first line of defense by seeing or hearing any advancing enemy and warn the main body of troops. There were a few of these LP's positioned around the perimeter wherever we were camped each night. Three men were used so that one man would be awake and alert while the other two could sleep, and shifts were taken. No smoking or light of any kind was allowed, and no talking unless absolutely necessary. When we first got to the LP site, I contacted our Mortar Company and gave them the coordinates of our location, and had them fire a test mortar round one hundred meters in front of our position. I did this again for one hundred meters behind our position to verify our location. This was the real test for the exercise we spent so much time on in training to find our individual hundred meter distance step count. If we miscalculated our location from miscounting steps or misreading the compass, we could be killed by our own fire. Usually after that mortar bracketing procedure was completed we were ready to begin or LP, but I had them fire another set of mortar rounds fifty meters in front and rear of our position. This completed we began our LP for the night. I wound up going out on two additional LP's, and was satisfied. The morning after the third LP we returned to the unit and had morning Mess. After we finished I was summoned to see the Company Commander in his command tent. I had not met the commander yet, and I thought he just wanted to meet me. Captain Simmons was a large, serious looking black man that had been a Sergeant E-7 in the Korean War, and became an officer afterward and was now commanding a company. He told me that a few of the men I had been on LP duty with complained that I was calling mortar fire in too close to the LP's. He first asked why I was even going out on LP's, platoon leaders didn't have to go out on LP's because of their rank and position. And asked why the close mortar fire. I told him the reason I went out was to gain experience fast and get close to the men, and the reason for the close mortar fire was in case we were about to be overrun by the enemy, I could call into the Mortar Company for support and tell them to drop fifty and the mortar rounds would hit the LP where we had been, since we would have been moving to the rear by then. The time saved not having to bracket the mortar rounds, (having the mortar rounds adjusted a little in one direction, then a little in another direction until the target is eventually found) would save our lives. Hearing this explanation and sizing me up, Captain Simmons told me to be careful, and said "carry on." The results of this meeting got back to the men in my platoon, and relationships and attitudes with the men started to improve. Over the following days I saw the men were believing in my ability to lead, even my platoon sergeant.

I forgot to mention there was another item of the uniform that members of our unit were authorized to wear. That item was a black silk scarf that was worn around our necks and under the collar. On the scarf we had our unit number embroidered. The wearing of the scarf was awarded to our battalion as a result of a major encounter with the enemy at the beginning of the conflict, where a large cache of black silk material was discovered. The material would have been used to make the black pajama uniforms for many Vietcong soldiers. Loss of this material was crippling for them at that time. Wearing the black scarves set us apart from every other soldier fighting in Vietnam, and made our battalion stand out from all others. The other distinction that set our Division apart was that all other units fighting in Vietnam had their unit arm patches blackened to camouflage the uniform, but not ours. The red one on our unit patch was never blackened out. It is said "If you're gonna be one, be a Big Red One!" The "Fighting First" was how were were known. The field soldiers in Vietnam didn't wear insignia depicting rank because the enemy would try and target the high ranking officers and sergeants, in order to weaken the fighting units strength. For that same reason we didn't use titles for the Officers and sergeants, instead we used number call signs associated with our positions. My call sign was 7-1, which meant I was the first platoon leader.

When we were in base camp our meals were in the Mess Hall, and we would get a tray and get in line to be served just like in school cafeterias. What every man usually did at some point was to pocket a small bottle of hot sauce that was always on the table with the salt and pepper. This was not stealing. It was put on the table for us, and to save the Mess hall personnel time and trouble for delivery, we would put it in our field packs and take it on missions. This was not a benefit, it was a necessity to make the C-Rations edible. The C-Ration kits contained a P-38 which was a finger held little piece of metal with a cutting edge to open cans. The kits contained a can of some type of potted meat, or a pasta with a meat sauce, or baked beans with small hot dog pieces, or ham and Lima beans for the main course. The regular C-Rations had some sort of date or banana bread that we either traded or gave away. But if you got the C-B1A kit, that type had fruit cocktail for the dessert. We didn't see the B1A's often.

To make the main meal more appetizing, and if it wasn't dark out yet, we would take a small piece of C-4 explosive from the block of C-4 and place it in an empty C-Ration can with slits cut in it, then light the C-4. We would place a can of whatever we wanted to warm up on top of the flame. Of course the use of C-4 was not found in the Army manual, and the practice was frowned upon. But doing the warm up and then dousing with the hot sauce made dinner so much better. And the reason we couldn't do this if it was dark was because no fires or lit cigarettes were allowed since they could give your position away. That would be a very good target for "Charlie."

The grunts, another name for an infantryman, who are in the field on operations for more than three days had an additional type of box dropped that contained toothbrushes, shaving cream and razors, and even packs of cigarettes. The packs of cigarettes only held three cigarettes, and the box looked like the ones that had candy cigarettes we had as kids. These were welcomed supplies, especially by the guys that smoked, and most did.

MONSOONS AND ANTS

The time we spent in the field presented many special experiences for us, such as the weather. Vietnam is hot year around, and the section of the country where we were near Saigon, had Monsoon season May through November. The heaviest downpours were in June, July and August. The rain doesn't last long but it dumps a lot of rain when it does. During this rainy period pushing through the terrain on our "Search and Destroy" missions, (changed to "reconnaissance in force" in order to be politically correct), we went through areas that had over four feet of standing water accumulate in less than an hour of rain fall. We had to carry our rifles over our heads because the water was over our shoulders, and we were praying we wouldn't step into a hole, or encounter an exotic snake.

Another incident occurred while on a different S&D operation. We were going through extremely thick vegetation and got caught up in a large stand of bamboo that was very dense and slow to cut our way through. The bamboo shoots were about two inches apart and we weren't making any progress. Then all of a sudden shots opened up on us at our front. Everyone hit the dirt and took up defensive firing positions. But after only a couple of minutes men started to yell in anguish, jumping up and letting their weapons land on the ground. Puzzled at first I soon realized that the bamboo had nests of red fire ants, and the stings or bites were so severe that the men under enemy fire would rather take the chance of getting shot rather than be bitten by the fire ants. It was fortunate that all of us were not attacked by the ants, the men that didn't have the ant encounter only had to fight off the Vietcong. After refocusing we were able to put down the aggression without taking any casualties, except for the guys that had dropped their weapons and suffered with welts all over their bodies from the fire ants. With all of our equipment and weapons gathered together, we headed back to base camp.

Then there was the time the weather and terrain caused our point men to miscalculate our position, and we actually wound up over the Cambodian border. This was a big f**king deal. We crossed over the border, and in a country we weren't fighting with. We were not allowed to be in Cambodia. Right after we realized the mistake, we happened upon a North Vietnamese Regular Army encampment, but something was different. They didn't seem to be on duty, they were quite relaxed. We figured it wasn't a base camp, it was an R&R camp and they were there for "Relaxation and Recreation." While deciding what to do, we were discovered and the decision was made for us, all hell broke loose. We were severely outnumbered but had the advantage of having our weapons with us at the ready, they had to scramble for theirs. It turned into a major firefight, and we couldn't call in any air support for help and cover, because we weren't allowed to engage the enemy in another country. When it was over we couldn't report the battle results, again because we were out of country. We were able to withdraw back into Vietnam and get some distance between us and the Cambodian camp before dark, so we made a quick camp for the night. The area we made camp had two inches of water on the ground and the rain continued. Our sleeping position was sitting back-to-back holding each other supported, and sitting in the pond that was forming. It promised to be a long night.

In the morning we woke up to a huge commotion, there were men pulling down their pants, taking off their shoes and socks, and generally freaking out. After sleeping in more than two inches of water the entire night, we were infested with hundreds of leeches, and they were getting pretty full by then. For those that aren't familiar with a Leech, it is a worm type organism that is small enough to penetrate clothing fabric, small enough to fit between the threads of the material. When it gets to the skin it latches on with its mouth and sucks blood until it is full, then it falls off. Yes, it is as disgusting as it sounds. We lit our cigarettes and used them to burn off the leeches that couldn't be pulled off. We also discovered what the phrase "I got your back" meant, because the men had to pull the leeches off each others backs. For days I still felt I had leeches on me.

We spent anywhere from three days up to two weeks in the "Bush" which was a field operation. The big Red One had a Division policy that when a unit was in the field we would get at least one hot meal. Whatever meal it was would be dropped in "Cambro's," which were insulated food containers. That promise could not be fulfilled only three times that I can remember, and that was because of heavy fire to the delivery helicopter. It was deemed too risky to make the drop. Anyway at least one of those times the meal was breakfast, and we all really hated missing that drop because it would have had real scrambled eggs. Instead we had to eat C-Rations, and the contents in the cans marked scrambled eggs were inedible.

One of the most emotional times in my life was after I arrived in country and we lost the first man of our Company. Seeing this in person when we were in the field really affected me emotionally and also in my mind. Many of us had seen relatives or friends dead in funeral parlors, but most, if not all, had never seen a man shot dead in front of us. Later that week we had a Memorial Service in a clearing at our base. The soldiers boots, helmet, rifle with black scarf tied around the rifle were set up next to two identical markers configured the same way. We lost three men that week. During the entire service with Taps playing and the gun salute, my body felt as if it would burst trying to deal with the extreme level of emotion I experienced. My problem was that this scenario would be played out too many times over the following weeks and months.

Orders came down to get our gear together and load the trucks, which were semitrailer trucks that we climbed up and filled like cattle. The trucks could hold thirty or so men. We drove to the landing strip where a Chinook CH-47 was there with its two large blades already spinning. This large "Chopper" was used for troop movement or supply delivery, could hold more than thirty soldiers fully equipped. We were using this one helicopter to transport an entire platoon instead of the usual five HU-1 choppers. We did not land into a hot LZ, but we didn't have to go far before we made contact and engaged in a brisk firefight and found ourselves pinned down by a sniper in the far tree line. I caught a flash of light from his rifle after he shot, and tried using my tracer rounds to direct fire for the grenadier to fire a round from the M-79 into that tree. He wasn't able to follow my tracers, so I took his M-79 and made the shot. That shot missed so I fired a second shot close to the first and took out the sniper. Now that we could move again we continued with the mission, and soon finished the firefight. Later when we returned to base camp the grenadier was sited for taking the sniper out and saving lives, and he later received the Army Commendation Medal.

Our enemy was called a variety of names. They went by "Vietcong," "Victor Charlie," "Charlie," "VC," "or "Cong," and fought their Gorilla warfare using tunnels and villages to hide in. The Vietnamese resistance was made up of regular people who had regular jobs like farming, or working in shops. This soldier had no formal military training and usually wore a uniform of loose fitting black silk pajamas. There wasn't any way to tell a combatant from a friendly local, unless you were engaged in a firefight with him. After the Vietcong initialized the attack, they would try to cause us harm then would pull back after we advanced. They would put snipers in trees to shoot at us intermittently, and waited until they had a killing shot. After one firefight we were checking the dead Vietcong bodies and identified one we recognized, he had been the barber. He was cleared through the base camp gate daily to go to work in the base barbershop. He was considered a Friendly, but in this case he was the one that gave information about our layout prior to the attack.

Then there was the North Vietnamese Regular Army, the professionally trained soldiers. When they engaged in battle it was was with a greater force of men. They were trained to tactically position their soldiers in strategic fighting and shooting placements. Another difference we discovered was that when the Regulars attacked they would let out blood curdling screams as they came charging at us. I remember discussing it with my men the first time I saw that happen. We came to the conclusion that they were all high on something to give them courage. Who knows, all we knew was that we were fighting an enemy that were nice enough to let us know when they were going to charge. Those screams did freak us out until the shooting began, then our automatic reactions and responses kicked in.

MIA

Following one lengthy firefight deep in the boonies, we were not able to account for one of our men in the third platoon. The platoon had already searched the area where he was last seen, with no success. The platoon leader went to inform the Captain. The Captain upon hearing this information got all of the platoons together, and had us stretch out along the entire firefight area. I suggested that we use the "Pershing Wedge" formation in case we were to encounter enemy fire while performing our search. Captain Simmons agreed. The "Pershing Wedge" was first used by General Pershing during World War II. It had the men further out on each flank start advancing first, and the man next to them be a few steps behind, then the next man be a few steps behind the previous man, and so on until there was one man in the "V" or wedge in the middle at the bottom. This formation could be shifted quickly in case we were fired upon, but this time we went without contact.

We continued the search well past the area the firefight took place without finding the missing man, nor any traces of his equipment or belongings. When the Captain was satisfied we had gone far enough to be sure the area was covered, he stopped the forward motion, had us turn around, and head back over the same area we had just searched checking for the missing soldier again. We repeated this twice more before it started to get dark. We got the order to make camp and send out "LP's," Listening Posts. When it got light the following morning we resumed our search. We needed to be absolutely positive every effort was made to find our missing man. "We will not leave one of our men behind," was what the Big Red One believed. But after hours of additional searching it was determined all efforts were exhausted, our soldier was declared "MIA" Missing In Action. Even though no trace of him was found, we were leaving him with the enemy. Alive, wounded, or dead we didn't know, but we did know there was nothing else we could do. We felt helpless, and prayed for him.

It was mid afternoon and we just got set up with our bunkers and my platoon had perimeter guard duty. The temperature was in the nineties, although it's always in the nineties. We were sweaty from filling sandbags, and all of a sudden a rain storm came up and we were getting drenched. We reacted quickly. We grabbed a bar of soap and stripped. All soaped up and the rain stopped as fast as it had started. We were quite a sight standing there wet, soapy, and naked, but fortunate. The rain started again and lasted until we had a good rinse. Later that same day it got stranger, three Vietnamese youngsters showed up carrying a bag of French style baguette loaves, and bottles of "33" brand Vietnamese beer on ice. Of course we were on our guard because the age of the enemy can start when they begin to walk. There might have been a hidden bomb or they could have had weapons. After we felt safe we made a purchase from them, what a treat, the bread had flecks of dirt in them, but was delicious, and the beer was cold and refreshing. Never figured out where the kids came from since there wasn't any village close by, but even in the boonies they knew where we were.

Sometimes things happen at the wrong time, as was the case the day we were at our outpost base camp standing in the chow line for lunch that was located outside in the center of the camp. We heard loud mortar fire approaching our perimeter, and the rounds were dropping within one hundred-fifty meters from us in the chow line. I had been standing in line waiting to be served, I was hungry and I really didn't want to lose my place in line. A few of us calculated that "Charlie" wouldn't be able to bracket the mortar hits before we got served. I was right, we got our food, and ten minutes later they hit the chow line that had been abandoned. Lucked out again.

Since Vietnam had been under the control of France for years, the Michelin Rubber Company had developed large investment stake in Vietnam with their massive rubber plantations. Our operations sector was the prime growing area for rubber trees and we would pass through acres of rows of the trees. Each tree would have a four inch shallow bowl affixed to the tree to catch the white rubber sap from the cuts made in the tree. Once collected it was processed, and eventually became tires. The process was similar to that of our northern maple tree sap collection to be made into maple syrup. At times we would engage in firefights in the long rows of trees with each man seeking cover behind a tree. At times we would have injured that needed to be flown out by a Medivac helicopter. To permit a "Chopper," helicopter to have enough space to land we would cut down, or blow down using C-4 explosives a number of the rubber trees. Each time we did this it was necessary to count the number of trees cut down or destroyed and report the number to command headquarters. The reported number was used to calculate the cost the United States had to reimburse Michelin Rubber for the loss. I was told the cost per tree was around fifty dollars, and we cut down a lot of trees. Besides cutting down trees to establish "LZ's," or Landing Zones for the helicopters, many trees were destroyed from the use of Napalm. Napalm was used to clear large swaths of land by burning it, this was to take away cover for the enemy. Also Agent Orange chemical was used to kill the fast growing thick vegetation, which probably affected the growth of the rubber trees.

During the third week in country I traded my M-16 rifle in for a shorter, faster firing M-15 rifle. The reason for this was I found I rarely fired my weapon in a firefight except to direct my fire for where I wanted my men to shoot. I only carried tracer rounds that were tipped with White Phosphorous. The round was the same size and power as used in the M-16, but the phosphorous would burn off while in flight showing the path of the round. When needed I would yell to the men to follow my rounds, I would then send a burst of three rounds into the spot I wanted their fire. I found this to be a very effective tool. I also started carrying a 45 caliber pistol, mostly as a back up weapon. I actually had three weapons, the M-15, a 45 caliber pistol, and a radio operator that kept me in touch with my Company, the Mortar Company, and the Artillery Company.

When we were in the field on an operation my radio operator was by my side at all times for the communications, but also because the hand microphone on the radio had a short curled cord that was attached to the twenty pound AN/PRC77 radio strapped to his back. My radio operator was unique. Every time we would stop to take a short break, or our forward progress was interrupted for any reason, he would fall asleep. Thankfully he would wake up quickly when it was time to proceed. Even in a firefight, when he would take cover sitting behind a tree or lay on the ground, within minutes he would be fast asleep, unbelievable! There was one skirmish we got into, and he was shot on the right side of his head. But since he was wearing his steel pot helmet and it didn't hit straight on, it was deflected and just dented the helmet and shook him up quite a bit. But wouldn't you know, it wasn't ten minutes later before he was asleep again! Retelling this story always gave us a good laugh, but in retrospect that was probably how my radio operator's mind dealt with the stress, or maybe he had narcolepsy.

In the same way I had been assigned to lead the First Platoon in the beginning, and how I had to wait to meet my men after they returned from a field operation, was how we met new personal joining up with our platoon. When we came back from the field to base camp, sometimes there would be a "FNG," or men that would be joining us. On three different occasions I was asked by my CO (Commanding Officer) if I wanted the new Lieutenant that had just arrived. He asked because at the time the Third Platoon needed to fill the platoon leader position. I asked Captain Simmons what the officer's MOS was and he said he majored in music, I asked him to send him to the other platoon!

We spent the day filling sandbags and using them to build bunkers in the process of setting up a forward base camp perimeter. The bunkers were built in a large circle and were constructed by digging a large hole and using the dirt removed from the hole to fill sandbags. When enough bags had been filled they were stacked three or four high on the sides and around the hole, leaving an opening in the back for a man to enter. On the front there were shooting ports, and the roof of the bunker was sandbagged also. We had to go through this drill every time we established a different forward base camp. At night we would sleep or keep watch on top of the bunkers or behind them, never inside. Nobody went inside the bunkers unless all hell broke out because Vietnam had a little snake that liked the bunkers too. It was called a Bamboo Viper, and was very poisonous.

The following day my platoon went on a Search and Destroy operation, with the other platoons staying behind to secure the camp. Upon our return hours later we split up and went to the bunkers we built the previous day. A few minutes later a couple of my men came running to my bunker and said there was someone hiding in their bunker and wouldn't come out. Several of us gathered around their bunker with rifles in hand. As we surrounded the bunker opening, we shouted for him to come out. We even tried using the few Vietnamese words we knew to try and coax him out. No success. We couldn't get too close because he was probably armed, so we couldn't see into the dark bunker, but we did hear him moving. Finally, I told everyone to take cover, then had someone throw a grenade into the bunker. After it exploded I sent one of the men in to drag him out. Were we surprised when he started dragging out a thirteen foot Boa Constrictor. Of course news of this dead prisoner circled the camp, and lots of photos were taken with the snake. The men that were assigned to the bunker said they were relieved, until I told them these snakes travel in pairs, which meant one was still out there. Nobody slept that night.

Intelligence reported there was enemy activity in our operational sector, and battalion briefed Company C and Company D commanders, and to formulate a plan to address the situation. When they returned Captain Simmons told the platoon leaders we would trek thirteen kilometers from base camp to engage a battalion sized contingent of North Vietnamese Regulars that were in the process of digging in. Within an hour we were on the move to that destination. It was the usual daytime temperature, hot, but it was dry, and our progress was going well. The route we were following took us through thick lush tropical vegetation, and all of a sudden we would pass behind a family's hut home. We liked going through a family yard because there were lots of different things growing, such as bananas, papayas, mangoes, and a fruit we called "Num Num's". The "Num Num" fruit reminded me of litchi's, and when the skin was peeled off the little ball of soft fruit inside was so sweet and delicious. So whenever we passed a tree of them everyone would grab a handful while passing by. We knew that this was stealing, and we shouldn't have done it. But we took them and really enjoyed them on that hot day.

We had traveled about ten kilometers to the edge of a stand of rubber trees when we had a mortar round hit right in front of us hitting and wounding a few of our men. Our medics rushed to them immediately and started attending to their wounds. The medic in my platoon was a conscientious objector. He did not agree with any part of the Vietnam "Conflict," but he still had to serve in the military. He made the choice not to carry or shoot a weapon, but was a brave and gutsy small wiry guy with a good disposition, and was liked by us all. We didn't share his views, but he didn't run off to Canada to avoid the Draft like many others did. After that first mortar round hit, shooting from the front and both sides ensued, and then mortar fire continued landing all around us. Returning the fire, and constructing three offensive fronts, we were eventually able to control the firefight. We were at a disadvantage since Charlie had been digging in building bunkers and had us in a crossfire. We were taking on casualties and our firing lines were getting strained from the loss of the wounded man and the one or two men that attended him. The battle lasted for hours and finally wound down with the help from artillery fire power causing the enemy to withdraw. After the shooting finally stopped we got busy surveying our damage, and set up a perimeter in case there was a following attack. At this time members of Company C and Company D were overlapping each others sector trying to help with the wounded and the dead. The commanders already had rubber trees being cut down to bring in the Medivac helicopters for the wounded. As I was going man to man I came upon my friend from Sergeant training in Fort Polk, Louisiana, Joe Black. He was down, but alive. I knelt down next to him and saw he had a chest wound and was struggling to breathe. He greeted me by just saying Fury, and forced a smile. I was attempting to comfort him when he asked me for a puff of my cigarette. Keep in mind we both had gone through extensive training for attending and treating the wounded, and we both knew smoking with any sort of wound connected with breathing was prohibited. Despite having that knowledge, I lifted his head up and cradled it in my arm, and took my cigarette, and held it to his mouth. This seemed to me like a scene right out of a Hollywood war movie. It only took one puff to discourage any more drags of that cigarette, the cough it produced proved to be too painful to have another puff. Joe said "Fury, it looks like I'm going home". When it was his turn to be loaded on to the helicopter, I squeezed his hand and said I will see you later.

Pay day was on the first of the month if we were at base camp to receive it. Base camp was anywhere in the Boonies that we filled sandbags, built bunkers, and set up a perimeter. We rarely got back to Battalion Headquarters Base where our proper assigned bunks were, unless we were on an operation close to the base. After a forward base camp was set up we would run S&D (Search and Destroy) operations that were usually thirteen or fourteen kilometers in length per day. One kilometer equals about two-thirds of a mile. In ninety degree plus heat, it was a grueling daily feat. Missing pay day a couple of days wasn't that big of a deal since we only had a few things to buy, and even fewer places to make a purchase. Cigarettes, beer, and soda were about the only items not supplied to us in the field, and most of my money was sent back to my wife in the States. I only kept twenty dollars a month, and was able to get by on that most of the time. Of course nearing the end of the month many guys would run out of money, because they found one more thing to spend their money on - gambling. There was a small percentage of the men in our platoon that would gamble whenever there was an opportunity and someone was always carrying a deck of cards. If you ran out of money before pay day, you could go to one of the soldiers that loaned money for a fee until you paid it back the next pay date. Yep, we had loan Sharks too!

We were not paid in dollars, we were paid in a colorful artsy bank note called "MPC'" or Military Payment Certificate. Everyone used the MPC, including the Vietnamese and those that were the enemy. The MPC was created to protect our currency from being misused. So in October 1968 the Military had a surprise redemption of all existing MPC at the same time, and a new series of MPC was issued, quite a logistics feat. This caught everyone that had been stockpiling illegally held MPC unable to unload them, and their MPC became worthless. A smart move for the Military.

A few weeks later I was told to report again to the CO. He just had another officer report in, but this time I had to take him, which meant I would be his platoon Sergeant now. After bringing the new Lieutenant to our hootch, he wanted to have a formation to meet his men. I took him aside and advised him to have the meeting inside the hootch instead of being an easy target for Charlie. He agreed. After that meeting was done, I suggested to him that he let me continue to run the platoon for a few days while he observed how the platoon operated. His response to me was he outranked me and he would run the platoon immediately. The Lieutenant had just graduated from OCS (Officers Candidate School), nicknamed "90 day wonders," and was pumped up. But in his nineteen years of wisdom I think he made the wrong decision. The very first firefight he was in he got killed from a snipers bullet to the head. What a sorry waste of a life, so young, so unnecessary. Upon his death I was placed into the platoon leader position again. After the Lieutenant was "KIA," Killed In Action, you would think I would have taken pause to sort out my thoughts and question my feelings and emotions. There was none of that process. I was accepting the loss of life, and not dealing with any emotions that came with death. After seeing men wounded and killed on nearly a daily basis, my feelings were suppressed. My reaction to these extreme events that don't occur in my civilian life were being handled as matter of fact events, and not stopping to dwell on the loss of life. I don't feel I had become insensitive. I think I just shut down in some way, just to be able to cope. Our wonderful minds have a way of protecting us by putting us on automatic pilot to allow us to continue to function.

FRENCH VILLA

I was given a mission when we were at our Battalion Base Camp to send a squad out for a forward listening post about six hundred meters from the base perimeter. I picked the men who were scheduled for the next assignment duty, and decided to accompany them. It had been raining hard the entire day, and it was now about an hour before dark and we were heading out. When we arrived to the location we had been sent, it was only about a hundred meters from a French Villa and a few out buildings close by. The French had a huge influence in Vietnam years before the Americans ever showed up, and they had their own ten year conflict with the Vietnamese. That is when their influence ended. Michelin Rubber is probably the largest French company in Vietnam and still depended on rubber tree sap production to make products such as tires.

The Villa we were close to was probably the plantation manager, and the out buildings were the homes of the plantation workers families. Before we set up our outpost, myself and two of my men checked out the closest hut. We knocked and pushed the door open, guns on the ready. We were surprised that the man inside motioned for us to come in, and we did. When we stepped in out of the rain he extended a can full of chopsticks toward us, and cupped his hand to his mouth as if eating. He was offering for us to join his family for dinner. We resisted, but he insisted.

Each soldier is an envoy for the United States, and expected to promote good will. His family was gathered in a circle around a few bowls of food on a cover on the floor. We took a quick taste of some rice and thanked them. We went back to the others and decided to set up the post right there on the mowed lawn of the Villa. With the heavy rain we couldn't see twenty feet in front of us, and we couldn't be seen either. In the morning we headed back to base looking and feeling like drowned rats. We didn't share any of the details from the night before.

I was called to report to Captain Simmons quarters where he told me another Lieutenant had been assigned to the Company. He said I would have to give up my position again because all of the other platoons had officers as platoon leaders. I thanked the Captain and went to greet the Lieutenant and take him to our platoon location. As with the last Lieutenant, I offered that he observe the platoon operation with me continuing to lead for awhile until he was comfortable with taking over. He agreed, which was good, but after three days he thought he was ready, and took over the platoon. Here we go again.

When the new Lieutenant took over we were already into the Tet New Year which started the beginning of February 1968. We had been getting intelligence reports predicting a large offensive from the North Vietnamese Army. We were back in Battalion base camp when we found out the intelligence reports were accurate. Word came down that helicopters would be picking us up in one hour, and were instructed to pack heavy, and that didn't mean to pack warm clothes and coats. It meant to gather all the ammunition we could carry. It was reported we were heading for a major battle located in Loch Ninh, which was Northwest of Saigon. When we were loading onto the helicopters, we found out we were going to land in a hot LZ. The Landing Zone was being fired upon from the tree line as the choppers landed. Since the entire Battalion was mobilizing and we only had a limited number of helicopters transporting men to the LZ, there had to be many separate troop drops. Once one load was dropped off the helicopters needed to head back and pick up the waiting load.

As the helicopters approached the Landing Zone, the Crew Chief would alert us to get ready, and when he gave the command to jump we were supposed to disembark no matter how far away from the ground we were. The helicopters could not afford to land, so the first and last guy off of the helicopter had the longest jump (or fall) to the ground, it averaged about eight or nine feet. The men in the middle would be the closest about two or three feet off the ground, but loaded the way we were even that shorter distance was not easy. Many jumping off the helicopter fell to the ground because of the load each was carrying and the uneven surface we landed on. But that was only part of the trouble, we were getting shot at from the time we came near the LZ. Once on the ground we were to leave the LZ fast and make it to cover at the edge of the clearing, paying attention not to run toward the field edge where the shooting was coming from. The first men dropped into the hot LZ had the hardest task since they were outgunned and were an easy target. The first men in had the most wounded, but as the helicopters dropped more and more men, Charlie was pushed back until they retreated.

We heard from Battalion that Tan Son Nhut Air Base, which was just outside of Saigon, and the air base most of us flew into from the States, was attacked on 31 January 1968. The North Vietnamese tried to get to our air power and resupply depot, but they were forced to withdraw. The base airstrips did sustain damage from mortar fire, but was repaired quickly to allow flights to continue.

After we cleared the Landing Zone we went directly to the area designated for the Battalion to set up the forward base camp. We started filling sandbags as soon as we arrived and established a perimeter, and since it was the whole Battalion, it was a big perimeter. While this was being accomplished, D Company was sent out in search of the enemy that had fired on the LZ earlier. At the same time all of the other platoon leaders in the remaining Company's went to the Battalion tent for a briefing. I stayed back with the sandbag activity because I was replaced by the new Lieutenant and was now Platoon Sergeant again. Sandbag duty continued all afternoon and we were making good progress, probably because we knew we would need the protection soon. A sense of urgency was evident throughout the camp. Everyone was getting prepared, for what, we didn't know as of yet. We didn't have to wait long to find out. We had been hearing a battle going on in the distance, and suspected it was D Company. Our location for our base camp was at the base of a hill that had a flatter area in the center, while each side of the hill was built up creating a sort of valley. If a perfect ambush site could be designed, this would be it, thick lush vegetation and shooting advantage from both sides.

BRING THEM BACK

The Lieutenant, our Platoon Leader, gathered us around to tell us what he found out at the briefing. He basically told us we were about to "hit the shit." Moments later the Lieutenant was radioed and told to send me to the command tent. When I got there, Captain Simmons said D Company was pinned down on the hill, and he wanted me to assemble a squad, get to their location, and bring them back. He showed me their location on my map, and said I had to get there now as they were running low on ammunition. He wished me good luck. On the way back to my men, I remember thinking the trust and confidence Captain Simmons had shown toward me ever since that day I explained the close mortar fire I brought around my Listening Posts. Maybe his favoritism towards me was from being a Sergeant in the Korean War, but it was probably just because he knew I had the best chance getting the task done.

I selected my best men and formed a squad, briefed them on the operation, loaded up with ammunition, and headed up toward the hill. The shooting we heard from camp was now getting louder as we worked our way up the hill. We really didn't need a map. I radioed the Major, D Company's commander, that we were approaching from the rear so he didn't think Charlie was surrounding them, and to prevent us getting fired upon. He acknowledged and frantically told me to hurry, the Company was running out of ammo. I told him we would be there in less than five minutes. On our way up the hill we passed through many bunkers that had been built into the hillside, but thankfully had been empty. This wasn't too strange since a lot of bunkers from previous battles had been abandoned by the Vietnamese. Knowing that we wouldn't use the bunkers, but that they might use them at a later date. We came up on D Company command location and went directly to the Major. I told him to follow the man I assigned to lead them back down to base camp while the rest of my squad would cover their return down the hill. The Major was surprised that only a squad was sent to help, but there wasn't time for discussion, and he gave the order to follow my man. My squad moved forward to the firing line while telling the guys we passed from D Company to follow the line of men down the hill. Action was heavy and we laid down a base of fire to cover the withdrawal. At first I think Charlie thought D Company had gotten reinforcements, because their shooting slowed, but that didn't last long. We soon started seeing the soldiers. They were North Vietnamese regulars and they were moving forward towards us. By that time the last man of the Company was on the path heading down. It was time for us to get out too. I called in the mortar fire on our position and said to fire for effect. We headed down the path and caught up to the last man in line, but it was going slower than planned because there were several wounded or dead that had to be carried down.

This put a wrinkle in my plan, I didn't want to be covering the withdrawal any longer than I had to, and I didn't want my men getting pinned down and us needing to be rescued. We stopped on the path and took up firing positions again, then we heard our mortar fire lighting up the location we had just left, and presumed overrun. We started to get shot at again, and we returned fire as we worked our way down the path. Every now and then we would spot a soldier, but we still had ammo and kept their advance checked. We were almost at the bottom of the hill and had caught up with the wounded being carried, but the decent was getting faster because men from base camp were meeting D Company at the base of the hill and helping with the wounded. The enemy advance was picking up steam with more shooting and more soldiers were being spotted trying to get to us before we made it down. I took a L.A.W. that one of my men brought with him. (A LAW is an M-72 Light Anti Tank Weapon.) It is a one shot 66mm round, a rocket within two tubes, one inside the other. The tubes would be extended to cock the weapon and fire it. You could not stand behind when firing because it had a back blast out the rear tube. The blast out the back would wound or kill a person standing there. I extended the tubes and warned everyone to clear themselves from the weapons back blast. I fired, the weapon misfired, after cursing, I tried firing again. This time it went off sending the LAW's round up the hill path and into the oncoming soldiers. The shot was effective I'm sure, but we did not hang around to watch. We made it the rest of the way down and into base camp, relieved.

I checked in with Captain Simmons, and my men went back to the platoon to regroup. When I got to his tent, he was already standing there with D Company's Major, and the look he had on his face was one of pleasure. Apparently the Major was recounting the mission to Captain Simmons, and both were pleased with the outcome. When he saw me he just smiled and said good job, thank you. The Major said said Thank You and shook my hand. I was dismissed, and went back to my platoon. I was later awarded the Bronze Star with "V" device. The V stood for valor, for returning D Company back to Base camp using only a squad sized force.

All through the night we would receive random mortar rounds hitting around the base camp, and a few saboteurs trying to breach our perimeter causing out-breaks of shooting and the firing of flares for illumina-tion. We did not get breached. Charlie was just looking for weak spots in our perimeter and he didn't find any. Because we went up the hill on the mission, we were excused from pulling perimeter duty that night. The fol-lowing morning C rations were breakfast, and everyone was busy working on their gear, and accumulating as much ammo as they could carry. At this time we hadn't been told if and when we would be heading out, but we knew the order would be coming, and soon. As planned Artillery barrages started hitting different areas on the hill with the idea we would just go up the hill after and survey the damage from the bombing. We learned from previous battles this wasn't what actually occurred. As soon as the Artillery barrages finished, we started get-ting hit with enemy fire and mortar rounds. The North Vietnamese were attacking our Base camp in our sec-tor. They sent a small force the size of a Company, and did cause damage by wounding a couple of soldiers. But the most damage was that Captain Simmons took a di-rect hit from a "RPG" round, Rocket Propelled Grenade, and because he was a large man, saved the lives of the men around him because he had taken the full impact of the round. We stopped the charge, and they retreated back up the hill. I went to Captain Simmons, and he was leaving us fast. His aid asked him who was to take over the Company, and with his dying breath said 7-1, my call sign. He had chosen me to command the Company. Right to the end he proved there was a special relationship we had shared. Captain Isiah Simmons was thirty-three years old, and died that day, 24 August 1968. He is remembered on the Wall on panel 46W, Line 008. I continue to miss him.

HILL 178

The order was given we were moving out in fifteen minutes. Our platoon leader already knew we would be following the second platoon up the hill again, and we now knew that this hill we had ascended to withdraw D Company the day prior was named Hill 178. This time it was different. The Lieutenant was in charge of the platoon, and I was in charge of the Company. Definitely not the typical leadership structure found in a military manual, but that was Captain Simmons last order. The formation we were using to ascend the hill was a wide sweeping side to side configuration, rather than the file behind one another like we had used the day before. We did not get far before we started to take enemy fire. The bunkers we had rushed around that were not occupied the previous day, were now occupied. Fierce fighting continued as we inched up the hill towards those bunkers until the North Vietnamese left them and moved up the hill to other occupied bunkers.

The slow advance continued for hours, despite the pounding the Artillery bestowed before we headed up the hill. The Cobra attack helicopters were still laying a heavy base of fire down as we made our advance. With all of our shooting, hand grenades being thrown, and mortar rounds being shot, we were still getting heavy enemy fire. This gives you an idea how fortified these bunkers were. We finally got near the top of the hill where the terrain was leveling out, and our front was getting less spread out, allowing our fire response to be more effective.

Within an hour or so after reaching that plateau the

fighting reduced, then ended. The North Vietnamese had withdrawn. Nobody thought for a moment the battle was over. We regrouped tending our wounded and dead, gathered ammunition, and intently watched forward for any movement. During this lull I was sought out by a Lieutenant Colonel from Battalion Headquarters, that had moved up to our company's position from the rear. He told me he was relieving me from Company Commander position and assuming the command. He said, "good job," and took command. I then went back to my platoon and once again to the platoon sergeant position. You almost need a program to keep track of who's in what position at any given time! There wasn't much lull time before another screaming attack occurred, and this time it seemed as if there were even more enemy soldiers. Maybe they had been waiting for reinforcements to reach their location. The fighting was hot and heavy, and I couldn't tell which side had the advantage. We were strung out in a wide front, but there weren't any holes. We had it covered well. As we were burning through our ammo, other men were bringing more to us from the rear, and we were also grabbing ammo from our fallen men. Then it happened, my platoon leader took off to our left flank with his radio operator, (my sleepy radio operator) because he said he saw some enemy. They left the rest of the platoon and went on their own, breaking up the front we had just formed. Damn. I told the squad leaders to maintain their position and stay engaged with the enemy. I grabbed a couple of men to accompany me to get the Lieutenant and bring him back. We had gone less than twenty yards when we saw the Lieutenant get shot dead. Now the situation had changed again. We needed to get to the Lieutenant, secure his body until we could bring him back, and protect the radio operator. That "John Wayne" action allowed our whole platoon to be put in a life threatening bind. We moved our position about fifteen yards to where the Lieutenant lay motionless, and we were still engaged with the North Vietnamese. In fact they saw what we were doing and were shifting their fire power to take advantage of our situation. Seeing them shift towards us, I had our men also shift the front line to the left flank, which brought them closer to us and provided more support. By this time the radio operator was back by my side, and I was once again the Platoon Leader, guarding over the Lieutenant's body. No man is ever left behind.

We could see the North Vietnamese soldiers and they could see us as shots were being traded, and then it happened. My right arm went flailing in spastic motions, and I felt a severe burning sensation in my chest and shoulder. I had just been shot by an AK-50 round, I knew it was an AK-50 rather than the more common AK-47 because I was engaged shooting at the soldier that had that faster firing AK-50. The round came from the same angle where he was, and my man next to me got a shot off at the same time he had fired and shot him. The shot hit me so hard that my helmet came off, and at first I thought my arm had been shot off. Within minutes my medic was crouched down beside me administering first aid, and at that time I realized I had been hit in the chest and did not suffer the loss of an arm. At this point I was pretty woozy and when they got me up to where the "Medivac," Medical Evacuation Helicopters were coming in, I was pretty wobbly also. When I got back to the LZ, no helicopters were landing because we were still experiencing heavy enemy fire, and there was only room for one helicopter to land. They couldn't take the chance of a helicopter being shot down in the LZ and preventing any other helicopter the ability to land. Finally the battle wound down somewhat, and the helicopters started to land and pick up the wounded. I was loaded onto the second or third one to land. They placed me on a stretcher and carried me to the helicopter where they placed the stretcher on an olive drab canvass hammock, on the third tier located on the back wall of the H-1D Huey Helicopter. The emergency field dressing my medic used had already bled through, and I was lying in a puddle of my blood. The crew chief was doing his best to keep me from passing out by urging me to keep my eyes open, and saying that everything was going to be fine.

LONG BINH

I am guessing the flight took fifteen or twenty minutes. When we landed we were greeted by a crew that removed my stretcher from the berth in the helicopter, and carried me inside the Second Evacuation Hospital, that was housed in tents rather than buildings. The hospital's mission was to triage all of the wounded in our sector and determine if the wounded would continue on to Long Binh hospital for surgery. The evacuation hospital location was closer to field operations, and was equipped to administer life-saving treatment not available in the field by a Medic. My wounds were cleaned and the dressings were replaced with new sterile ones. I was loaded back onto another helicopter and taken to the 93rd Evacuate Hospital in Long Binh.

Arriving at Long Binh the helicopter was greeted by a crew dressed in green hospital garments, and they placed the stretcher on a gurney and brought me into one of the Quonset Hut buildings. I was wheeled into the operating room. I can't remember exactly what happened in the operating room, except that they had to insert a chest tube into my right side. This had to done because I was told my right lung had collapsed and the cavity was full of blood. They made a cut in my side with a scalpel, and pushed a hard plastic pointed tube into my side between two rib bones, and into the space where my lung should have occupied. Believe me when I say that pain was far worse than anything I felt when I got shot, and I did let them know. After the tube was in and they saw it was working, I guess I was knocked out and operated on, because the next thing I remember was waking up in a clean hospital bed with real sheets feeling pretty groggy and plenty sore. The usual hospital activities consisting of bed pans, bandage changing, pills, etc. occupied most of my time lying in bed and falling in and out of sleep. I found out that the round that hit me went into my chest creating a small entry hole that just missed my heart, but did penetrate my lung causing it to collapse and fill with blood. The round then continued tumbling, as the military round was designed to do, exiting out my back by my right shoulder creating a much larger torn hole. The sutures used to close up the wound were made of stainless steel, the gauge size could have been used to mend fences.

On the third day in the hospital I was visited by a Red Cross representative wanting to leave writing paper and envelopes so I could write a letter back home to let my family know I was alright. I asked him to leave the materials and I would do it a little later. I had no intention of writing home with that news, because since the day I arrived in Vietnam I had been writing every chance I had. When I wrote that first letter I tried putting everyone, especially Mom, at ease by telling them I was working as a Quartermaster, distributing uniforms, sheets, pillows, and such. I said my job was in the rear back at Battalion Headquarters and I wasn't in harms way, although it was a dirty clay mess, which was to explain why the envelopes were dirty at times.

Well this tactic backfired on me since the Army notified my parents that I had been awarded the Purple Heart, given for being wounded in combat. I found out later my parents notified the Red Cross, who then notified the Army that they had not heard from me and they wanted to know why. I don't know how long it took, but a Big Red One Sergeant Major showed up at my bedside letting me know he wasn't happy that I didn't let my parents know I had been wounded. He arranged for me to be taken to another section of the hospital where a MARS radio station was set up, and had me place a call home using the HAM radio airways. After instructing Mom and Dad to say "over" after they stopped talking, it went well. They were just glad to hear my voice proving I was still alive. I told them I would write and explain everything in detail. I wrote, but not in detail, I only wrote as much as I felt was needed, I still withheld much of the information.

After getting to a healing point where a patient is ruled stable, the very serious injuries were sent to our military hospitals in Germany where they would either stay there and be treated, or sent to the States to be treated. The system worked, but the problem was that there were only a set number of spots available each week for evacuation out of the country, and since the Tet Offensive, there were many more injuries. So, because of the volume of injuries, only the very worse wounded were evacuated. A month earlier, an injury like mine would have been a flight back to the states and now they couldn't even send me to Germany. I was still lying on my back and confined to my bed when I heard the news that our First Division Commander's helicopter had been shot down over Loch Ninh while surveying the battle on Hill 178 where I had been shot two days prior on September 11. Major General Keith L. Ware commanded the First Division. He was fifty-three when he died Friday, September 13, 1968. My General had been awarded the

Medal of honor, Silver Star, and the Distinguished Service cross. He is now buried in Arlington Cemetery, and is on the Vietnam Memorial Wall in Washington, D.C., on panel 44W, line 055. Heavy anti-aircraft fire brought the helicopter down. Also perishing in the crash was his three command staff, four helicopter crew, and General Ware's white German Shepard. This was a crushing blow to our Division. Losing all of the top echelon staff of our Division was quite a victory for the enemy, and regrouping had to be done at once. I soon heard that General Orwin Talbott, also a two-star general, had taken command of the Division. The General had been on Utah Beach during D-Day invasion of Normandy, France in World War II. The Division was in good hands.

After a couple of weeks in the hospital the doctors told me they were going to remove my chest tube. I asked if they were going to give me a needle at the site for pain since it hurt so much when they put it in. Their response was no, and said don't worry, the pain doesn't nearly compare to that. Liars, it didn't hurt as bad as it did going in, but pain is pain. There must be a better method to perform that procedure. Several days later I was disconnected from all of my hookups, and was allowed to get out of bed. The first thing I noticed was the guy across the room lying prone in his bed, and all bandaged up. I made my way over to him and was surprised it was my friend Joe Black! He had been at the 93rd Evacuate ever since he got wounded, about a month prior to me getting there. He recognized me, but his speech was weak. He said the doctors were sending him back to the states as soon as he was stable. His chest tube was still in place so it would be a while. I felt bad for him, he looked so weak, and still needed to go through the chest tube removal pain. Three days later they did remove his chest tube, and I felt his pain. The following day he left for the States, and that was the last contact I had with him.

Entertainers, movie stars, and sports greats have always given support to our troops throughout our country's many wars, especially our hospitalized troops, and this conflict was no different. While I was confined to my bed we had some celebrities visit the hospital and they stopped by my bed for some photo opportunities. Gary Crosby, singer and actor, and son of Bing Crosby stopped by with another actor whose name I can't remember. Sebastian Cabot who was Mr. French on "Family Affair," and was in the movie "Kismet," also came by. The actor who starred as Wally on "The adventures of Ozzie and Harriet," Skip Young, dropped by too. Sharon Hillyer, who was known for her appearance in "Star Trek," and "Get Smart" also stopped by and left an autographed photo. The time and effort these individuals spend visiting and performing is so important to the recovering soldiers, and troops from all of the military services away from their home, families and friends, and means so much to them.

CAMERON BAY

When I was able to get around better, I was transferred to Cameron Bay to convalesce for a few weeks prior to reporting back to my unit. Cameron Bay was on the coast of Vietnam and consisted of many one level huts used for hospital wards, basically a large room that had a lot of bunks with patients recovering from various injuries. The huts were segregated housing Americans, Korean ally soldiers, and even Vietnamese civilians. All were recuperating from battle wounds, malaria, encephalitis, or other maladies. In peace time this location on the coast of the South China Sea could be a top tourist destination, with its white sandy beaches and tropical temperatures. During a monsoon storm, the seas got pretty rough and the waves were building, so some Air Force airmen stationed at Cameron Bay took to the water on their surfboards. A very unlikely site to behold in a war zone, but the surfboards were probably secretly flown in on one of our Air Force aircraft.

It took mail a long time to get back and forth from the States, and "Care" packages (goodies sent to us from home), took even longer. But they had the chance to catch up with us at Cameron Bay. One guy who got great Care packages had dried meat sticks called "Slim Jim's" that were sent every other week from his dad who was connected with the company, and he was happy to share with us! My Care packages consisted of all types of Italian treats. It seemed like Christmas whenever I had one delivered. There was one instance though that my family decided to step it up a little by putting a straw covered bottle of Chianti in the package. The thought was great, but the way it must have been handled caused the bottle to break and saturate all of the other items in the box. By the time I received the box it was completely dry, and everything inside was purple. We ate it anyway.

I hung out with a couple of good American companions, but also a Korean ROK Ranger that had been a movie director in Seoul, Korea during civilian life. In Korea, every man was required to pull a stint in the Army. When I asked why he thought Korea was fighting with us in Vietnam, his answer was immediate. He said they owed us since we came to their help for the Korean war, and were still there protecting them. The Koreans had their own barrack, and my friend brought me there to meet some of his friends. This was highly unusual. No Americans ever went into their hootch, and I did receive some raised eyebrows. There were a few groups of men playing a marble board game. I have no idea what it was called, let alone how it was played, but it was very popular among the Koreans. The ROK Rangers had a reputation for being a ferocious fighting force, and rumors say that after a battle they would sometimes behead the Vietnamese fighters. I don't know if that was a fact or not, but I do know the Vietnamese feared the Korean encounters. On the battlefield they were ruthless, but in their day-to-day lives I found them to be caring and sensitive people.

I'm actually fortunate to have spent the time in recovery at beautiful Cameron bay, since that was where I met another patient, who was a sergeant, who taught me how to play chess. While learning, I played many, many games with him as well as a few others that also knew how to play. I really enjoyed the competition, and was able to see my skills improve with each game.

When I was at the 93rd Evacuation Hospital, the hardest part was being around all of the severely injured soldiers. I would just start to know someone, then the following day they would be shipped back to their unit, shipped to Germany, or to the States, or worse die from complications. You could never escape the perils of war.

When it was time to remove the stitches, they needed to be removed with a needle nose pliers type of instrument that was able to cut the stainless steel stitches and pull them out of the skin tissue. I didn't expect the pain of the procedure. Granted the reason metal stitches were used in the first place was to hold the skin together, to close up some major holes in my chest and back. But cutting the stitches tore that little piece of healed skin at the base of the stitch where it went into the body. And as mentioned before, the stitches were of a sizable gauge, and were not as flexible as were the thread type that would come out smooth and straight. When each was pulled out with the pliers, there was pain for each one. I was glad when that was over. Funny thing though, for the next month or so, I would have little pieces of metal stitches work their way out of my skin at the entry holes of the stitches. There wasn't any pain associated with that, but it really felt very strange. Guess they didn't get them all out. Shortly after the stitches were removed I was notified I would be going back to my unit the following day. I didn't have much to pack up since I came to the hospital with only my bloody uniform that had been torn to shreds to gain access to the wounds. I was issued some other uniform items and a shaving kit to help me get through my hospital stay. In the morning I met with the jeep driver to take me back to my unit. I was classified healed enough to return to duty, but every bump we ran over on the way back jarred me enough to make me grimace from pain and grab my chest. Upon arriving to my unit in Lai Khe, I checked in with the Company First Sergeant. He informed me my platoon was here at base camp and I was to assume the first platoon leader position since I was the ranking "NCO'" Non Commissioned Officer.

RETURN TO THE FIELD

I was welcomed back by my men, and most were surprised to see me back. A few new faces were now assigned to our platoon and I needed to assess their fighting ability and skills. Things felt familiar but different coming back to the field. Primarily my advocate and friend Captain Simmons was gone, and a new Major was now commanding our Company. Besides that, a couple of my men had been killed, and I was briefed on the circumstances under how they had died. But the biggest difference coming back to the field was the fear I felt. It was hard to describe, I was questioning myself as to whether or not I could still have the confidence and mentality to perform as "Sgt. Fury." I felt the fear of taking another round to my chest, wounding or killing me. I was very much aware of my mortality after being shot, and would have to deal with it now. "Duty First," the First Division's motto, now had a new meaning for me.

The transition back to my platoon wasn't too difficult, but I did have to get used to my new radio operator. My previous radio operator, "Sleepy," that was reassigned to our Lieutenant who had gotten shot and killed, had served his year, left the country and went home. This was referred to "DROS," Date Returned from Overseas, and whenever anyone wanted to know how much time you had left to serve in country, they would just ask "when do you DROS?" It saved a lot of words.

In preparation for an upcoming operation, I was given the opportunity as the advance platoon leader, landing in the LZ to take a "LOH," Light Observation Helicopter, for reconnaissance and to scout the Landing

Zone area for layout, cover, and direction our platoon should move upon landing. Using the helicopter and seeing the actual layout of the potential firefight from the air gave me so much more perspective than just viewing the terrain map as I normally did. The nickname for this helicopter was "Loach," a play on "LOH." It was small and nimble and only held two men. The pilot had the front seat, and I sat behind him. The LOH landed near the platoon's location back at base camp. After leaving the aircraft I reported to our Company Commander and briefed him on what I had observed and how I planned to carry out the mission. With no objections to my plan, I was dismissed and went to my platoon to organize my men. The operation was a two-platoon sized force with my platoon leading the point. We were trucked to the airstrip and loaded onto a CH-47 Chinook helicopter. We were usually transported by the UH-1 Huey, but instead of using ten Huey's, we only needed two Chinooks. The Chinook was long and had a propeller in the front on the top, and one in the rear on top. It was rated to carry between thirty and thirty-five men in full gear. This day we would be pushing that limit slightly, jamming ourselves into every bit of floor space there was. Another reason we were using the Chinooks was that a friendly LZ was anticipated, so the chance of a major loss of men and an expensive helicopter was minimal this time. My men carried out their orders upon landing as discussed, and we regrouped inside the tree line after disembarking the helicopter. The two point men took up their positions and we began our reconnaissance-in-force operation.

I mentioned before the relentless amount of "humping the boonies" we did in the tropical heat. Well this operation had us humping thirteen kilometers to set up camp. For our safety, and for us not to be surprised by Charlie, we were expected to be at high alert at all times. Besides looking for enemy ambushes, we had to be on the lookout for trip wires connected to booby traps that would set off explosive charges in many different ways. We had to watch for dug pits that would range in size from a small foot-sized hole, to one that could easily accommodate a full-sized man. In the pits were usually sharpened objects such as bamboo stakes driven into the bottom of the pit, point side up, and covered with human feces. The Vietcong would place the booby traps along well traveled paths through the dense vegetation, so the U.S. Soldier would try to avoid these paths and cut a new path alongside the well traveled one. This was a safer strategy, but men will be men, and cutting new paths was slow and tiresome. The men had to be reminded constantly not to stay on the paths. Our progress after a couple of hours was slow because we had come upon a hole in the ground with a wooden door over it. This was not the first of these doors we had seen on our operations. It was a "Rat Hole," the entrance to an underground maze of intricate tunnels and connected rooms. The enemy used the underground to hide and recover from fighting, as hospitals, or escape from firefights with us. The Vietnamese were small in stature, so the tunnel openings were small too. Therefore the smallest man of our unit was usually the unofficial designated "Tunnel Rat." When a hole was found, we would place a guard on it while the rest of the men would search the area for other holes used for escape exits. We would then toss a smoke grenade into the entrance hole and watch for smoke or "VC" to emerge from the holes. After the smoke or VC came out, our tunnel rat would enter the hole to investigate its secrets. Caution was necessary here also, because the VC would booby trap the tunnels for our tunnel rats. Not a pleasant job: close quarters, dark, sometimes wet, and on top of that, needing to search for booby traps. I'm glad I wasn't the smallest guy! This search of the tunnels did not end up producing any prisoners, but we were able to determine from one of the rooms that they were using it for an emergency hospital. We confiscated weapons, field maps, and operation plans. The maps and plans would be forwarded to "S-1," our intelligence branch, to interpret and determine what the enemy's next battle move was to be. After we finished with the tunnel search and retrieval, we set explosive charges to destroy as much of the tunnel as we could. Many times we would find yet another tunnel branch that we did not uncover, but the explosion would give its location away.

Our operation's progress had been hampered by the tunnel project, and it was now late afternoon. We came upon a spot that had good fields of fire, and was clear enough to spot any movement over a hundred yards out, so we made overnight camp there. I sent out listening posts and assigned watch schedules. The other platoon set up behind us and made the same preparations. Sleeping was restless though, because there was a firefight that we could hear off in the distance. They were getting air support from "Puff the Magic Dragon," which was a converted AC-47 air-to-ground attack aircraft, that spewed out an immense amount of fire power with a couple of mini-guns that used the same round as the M-60 machine gun. The sound of the gun firing was terrifying, but the rain of thousands of rounds hitting the ground targets was devastating. The action we heard didn't make it to us, and we did not have orders to go to their aid.

The morning started off uneventful with our C-ration breakfast. Our operation continued after stowing our trash with our gear. We humped for about an hour when we started taking shots from a sniper up ahead. One man was hit immediately and went down. We took cover and returned fire while "doc," the medic, went to his assistance. Only minutes went by before a full blown firefight ensued, after the snipers' shots alerted the rest of the enemy contingent. We were now taking intense enemy fire, and I was waiting for the artillery fire I had called in and requested. Within ten minutes the artillery barrage commenced, but since the rounds were landing well behind the enemy's location, it would only be effective when the enemy would try and withdraw. I could have called mortars in closer, but the artillery is so much more powerful and needs a little more distance, or else we would become the targets too. Nevertheless, the artillery did get the attention of the Vietcong, since their shooting at us drastically diminished.

I had called for a "Dustoff," a medivac helicopter, to lift off two men that now needed to get to the hospital, but we had to squash this firefight first. After a time we stopped getting fire, and the chopper was radioing that he was ready to come into the LZ for the pickup. We threw out smoke grenades to mark the LZ, and he came in and loaded the men. The medivac helicopter pilots were real heroes of the war. They spent almost every mission in harms way, performing most of the "Dustoffs" picking up the wounded under live fire. This had been the first enemy encounter, and firefight since I had been hit at Loch Ninh weeks earlier. I remember my first reaction when that sniper opened up on us. I was instantly at a high level of alertness, and I had a feeling shoot through my body of fear and dread that I had never felt before. Fortunately, the feeling was fleeting, and I was able to perform as expected.

The first soldier that was lifted out was "KIA," Killed in Action. He died on the helicopter while in route to the hospital. My other man was wounded, but it was minor, and he would be returning to the platoon in a few days with his Purple Heart award. We continued our operation until we concluded our initial objective having no further contact with the Vietcong. When we returned to our base camp everyone was anxious to stow our gear and get showers, since the two-day operation had turned into a six-day operation. Approaching our base camp we noticed a lot of activity directly in our path. The press corps decided to get some live footage for the evening news back home, filming combat soldiers returning from a mission after days in the boonies. As we approached the cameras a funny thing happened. The closer we got the more the cameramen backed away. After six days in the field sweating, laying on the ground, and having less than sanitary conditions, we were repulsive. The smell was not evident to us because we had gotten used to each others stench over the days. But the normally groomed individual couldn't handle it. So, we were able to continue to our hootch without having to give any interviews with the press. They only got their movie footage.

It had been seven and a half months since I arrived in country, but it seemed as if I had been in Vietnam for years. I think the reason for this is that I only had one job, one focus, one objective every day. There weren't any outside distractions like meeting family or friends for dinner or drinks, going to a movie, or planning a weekend getaway. The Army did provide the opportunity for a soldier to get away from the action for a few days after being in the field for several months. This was called "R&R" (Rest and Relaxation,) and the men that took the opportunity to use the pass usually went to Bangkok, Thailand, and a few went to Hawaii after making arrangements to meet their wives or girlfriends. More days off were needed in order to take the Hawaiian trip, and that was mostly impossible as R&R was allowed based on the troop strength in the units. The war had to be manned first, R&R was second. I did not take R&R, maybe because my hospital stay cut into my opportunity. And the bottom line was that I didn't keep enough money out of my monthly pay to fund a trip to Thailand.

One afternoon at Lai Khe base camp, I was called to report to the Sergeant Major at battalion Headquarters. When I walked in, there was the Company Commander, our Sergeant Major, and the Division's Sergeant Major. I was introduced to the Division's Sergeant major and told to take a seat. He said there was a new position as Liaison to the Division's General at the 93rd Evacuation Hospital in Long Binh, and he wanted me to fill it. He explained my position as Liaison would place me in charge of every man from the First Division, as well as every man in units under operational control of the Division, such as the 11th Armored Cavalry and Robin Hood, the helicopter unit. My command over these men was only while they were in the 93rd Evacuation Hospital. I would tend to their non-medical needs, such as provide writing paper, and contacting units or families back home. The Sergeant Major concluded saying that I had until the following morning before he left to make my decision. I thanked him and went back to my hootch while my mind went crazy. As unbelievable as it might seem, leaving the field meant leaving my men, and I was finally getting comfortable with my combat leadership roll again. On the other hand to get a deliberate visit and job offer from the Division's Command Sergeant Major was quite an honor, and the following morning I sent word that I accepted the position.

DIVISION LIAISON

The Battalion jeep driver gave me a ride to Long Binh, to the 93rd Evacuation Hospital. It was strange coming here since the last time I was here I had been delivered on a stretcher by helicopter, and headed to the operating room. Ironically, now I was assigned to oversee wounded soldiers, just as I was, that would arrive in the same way by helicopter. I reported into the hospital commanders office, presented my orders, and was directed to where my hootch was located. The hootch was a single level building made of wood with a galvanized roof. It was divided into six room, one for each sergeant liaison from five other divisions other than mine. It turns out I was joining a very unique group that was assigned to the commanding officer of the 93rd Evacuation Hospital, but only answered to the separate divisions that each sergeant represented. As a Sergeant E-6, I was not the ranking sergeant in our hootch. That distinction went to the Sergeant E-7 from Guam that was with the 101st Airborne Division. Every one of the sergeants were there because of different circumstances and reasons, but all were liaisons to their divisions. The workload of the others was lighter than mine simply because the 93rd was located in the 1st Division's area of operations. The other sergeants would oversee any wounded transferred here from other parts of the country for treatment.

I got settled in my room and met some of the sergeants I would be sharing the building with. I was surprised that the room was a real room with walls, but no door - this would work. During the next week I began to learn what was expected of me in order to join in this new social environment, and live with these seasoned career sergeants, "Lifers". As mentioned before, each sergeant reported only to their respective Division Commander, but we were still subject to barrack inspections by the 93rd Evacuation Hospital Commander. Because of that it was our individual responsibility to keep our rooms and general barrack area inspection-ready at all times - not a problem. Next, each of us was expected to kick in a few dollars each month to pay for a "Mama-san," a Vietnamese middle aged woman that had been cleared to come through the security gates of the hospital to perform day work at our hootch. Our Mama-san would clean our building, wash bedding and dirty uniforms, starch and iron our uniforms, and shine our extra pair of boots, all for about thirty dollars per month. Other barracks that hired Vietnamese workers chose to hire the young pretty girls instead of a Mama-san, for the obvious reasons, but my barrack sergeants wise in their years of experience knew where to get the best value. For instance the young girls required their bosses to supply them with several cans of spray starch purchased from the "PX," Post Exchange store, that cost a few dollars a can. Our Mama-san made her own starch from rice, and it didn't cost us anything. The young girls didn't work as hard, and tired easily, and charged extra for polishing each pair of boots. We definitely had the best employee. Our ability to communicate with our Mama-san was limited, to say the least. We knew a handful of Vietnamese words, none of which would apply to domestic chores we wanted her to accomplish, and she knew even less English. Despite this lack of verbal communication, we were able to let her know what we wanted her to do.

Sometimes we would try to joke with her, and would at times reach the point she would laugh, instead of yelling back at us like she normally did.

A few days after arriving at the 93rd Evac, my Sergeant Major of the Division visited with me again, but this time he brought two cases of mixed brand cigarettes. He told me they were for the Division's men brought into the hospital, and if I needed more before he returned, all I had to do was call. We then took a tour of the wards and that time only four soldiers from our unit were being treated. The Sergeant major talked to each man letting them know that we take care of our own; pointing to me saying, Sergeant Myles will take care of anything you need. After the tour I accompanied him back to his helicopter, and he headed back to Headquarters.

This marked the day that my wheeling and dealing, bartering and trading era in the Army began. My thoughts went back to the television sitcoms like Sergeant Bilco, or the more recent MASH series, where anything could be acquired if you had something of value to trade. I now had that item of trade, and apparently with a never ending supply - cigarettes!

I had a double locker in my assigned office space in the hospital, and that is where I stored the cartons of cigarettes. The mix that the Sergeant Major delivered had brands like Lucky Strike, Pall Mall, Camel, and Chesterfield brands that some still smoked, but not the majority. So I formed a relationship with the PX sergeant. I gave him all of the off brands, and he would exchange them for cartons of Marlboro, Winston, and Salem. We negotiated a fair exchange rate of an extra carton or two of the off brands for the popular ones. I met with him after sorting each new delivery of cigarettes. And I was building quite a stash, even after dispensing to any of my wounded, and supplying one of the sergeants in my hootch Winston's, and of course feeding my own habit for Marlboro's. None of the other Liaisons were given anything from their divisions. On my daily rounds of the wards I would visit with the men from my division, making sure their requests were always taken care of, and if they smoked, gave them the brand of their choice. I supplied them with writing paper and made telephone calls for them, as well as anything else they asked of me. Of course while visiting my men, there would be a patient in the next bed that didn't have Liaison representation from their unit at the hospital. So I would sort of adopt them and give them cigarettes also. I kept a small book in my uniform pocket recording who I had on the wards, their unit, cigarette brand, and any other information I had pertaining to them. Many of the men I helped that weren't in my division were so grateful for the favors, they offered to repay my kindness with services they were able to supply. The Lieutenant with the Robin Hood Helicopters, under operational control of the Big Red One, offered me a helicopter trip anywhere at any time. This information went into my book. Some patients weren't in positions to offer anything to trade, but were very grateful anyway. The smokes didn't cost me anything, and we were all in the same boat!

Another use I found for the cigarettes was to barter for bottles of liquor and cases of beer with the PX, but the exchange rate was a little steeper. I also made a connection with the Mess Hall Sergeant who smoked Salem. I was able to trade cigarettes for twenty-five pound bags of flour or rice, a case of tomatoes, spices, and anything else I might need to make homemade pasta meals right in our hootch. There was one instance where a large concrete truck was passing our hootch when we were standing outside having a beer. I waved the truck down and asked where he was heading. He said he was going to the hospital commander's residence to pour a driveway. I convinced him to stop at our hootch on his next run and drop his load for ten cartons of cigarettes. We hustled to gather some lumber and quickly framed out a patio in front of our hootch. When he returned he dumped his concrete load, and we formed our new patio - the only one on the base other than the commander's. Now that we had a patio, we of course needed a grill, and within a couple of days we somehow had that built too.

I didn't spend much time and effort decorating my room in the hootch, because except for the surprise inspections, nobody would see it but me. I did want to sleep in comfort, so I acquired some green bedding from the operating room linen storage. The green bedding seemed cooler than the white stuff we were issued, but I couldn't let Mama-san wash those and hang them out to dry. When I needed fresh linens, I just carried them back to the operating room area and picked up a new set of bedding. Another improvement I made to help me sleep better, was to rid the fear of the gigantic roaches and spiders that would sometimes fall from the ceilings at night. I came across a parachute while on my hospital travels, and I made a huge canopy that covered my room's entire ceiling. I actually could have covered three rooms, but I didn't. Instead my room looked like a scene out of the Arabian Nights.

My social life was with the Sergeants in my hootch. We all liked to eat and drink, and we did a lot of both. One gathering in particular was special when our sergeant from Guam's friend Sergeant Tito, from the Corps of Engineers (and also from Guam), brought us a Seika deer for us to cook. While Sergeant Tito was on the bulldozer in the jungle clearing land, he shot the Seika deer with his bow and arrow. We had our grill fired up and hot when he arrived. I had cooked a large pot of rice from my room pantry, and the beer was cold. I can still remember how good that feast tasted, and the fellowship we all had that night.

Making my routine ward rounds one day, I stopped by to see the Vietnamese kids that were in the hospital with injuries from booby traps and land mines. Some of them had missing limbs, and bodies with scars that they would be carrying throughout their lives. One of the boys about twelve years old, was confined to the bed with his right leg elevated and in a sling. His leg had been pinned together and I'm sure he had a lot of pain, but I always caught him with a big smile on his face. On this visit I brought a pair of scissors and a comb with me, because I decided to give him a much needed haircut. He really liked getting a haircut, but I didn't think it through. When the other six kids saw what I had done, they wanted a haircut also. Understand, I never had any barber training, but I did give six more haircuts. When I finished cutting hair, I continued my ward rounds, and carried the kids smiles with me the rest of the day.

I was supposed to include the 11th Armored Cavalry troops in my care, because they were under operational control of The Big Red One. This pertained especially to the patient that came in one day, General George Patton, the commanding officer for the 11th Armored Cavalry. General Patton was the son of the World War II famous and decorated General George Patton. I was in awe of being in the presence of someone related to that war hero. The General Patton in front of me was in the hospital for an operation not resulting from a battle wound. The 11th Armored Cavalry Brigade consisted of "APC's," Armored Personnel Carriers, and tanks, and they supported us infantrymen with fire power from the tanks, and transported us at times through the jungle in a hurry in the APC's. When I went to greet the General he had already changed into a hospital gown and was laying in bed in the private room. After introducing myself, he gave me a few telephone numbers to call and messages to deliver. He also asked me to take his pistol, uniform, and wallet and hold them for him. I took his possessions and locked them in my office locker. General Patton stayed in the hospital less than a week, which gave me enough time to have his uniform cleaned and pressed and ready for his return to his unit(my Mamasan did this for me). When his adjutant Colonel arrived to take him back, he brought an 11th Armored Cavalry appreciation folder for the General to give me.

In addition to visiting with my unit's soldiers and passing out cigarettes, I was making friends with the medical personnel. One of the nurses in charge of the Emergency Room Triage noticed that I showed interest in the emergency care, so he offered to show me how to start an "IV," intravenous drip, in case triage got busy and I needed to step in and help. He opened an IV needle package and walked me through the whole procedure, having me use his forearm to practice. After some reluctance about possibly doing it wrong and hurting him, he said not to worry, because after I was finished, he was going to use my arm to practice. Thankfully, I started the IV without hurting him, and in turn he was gentle when he did mine. It turned out there was one instance when I was called upon to start an IV in the ER when they got overrun with wounded troops, and I was able to do it. Slower than an experienced nurse, but I did it correctly.

There was something I did when a wounded man from my old Company went into surgery. I was allowed to dress and go into the operating room to watch their operations. This was definitely not a requirement I was expected to perform, but for some reason I felt that I needed to be there with them while they were under the knife. Unfortunately I observed several of my company's soldiers operations for various battle wounds.

There was a short lull in my work load, since I only had one soldier in the hospital at the time. I made arrangements for one of the other Liaisons to cover my duties, and look after my soldier. I scheduled a trip to meet the Saigon Liaison for a couple of days. That sergeant had been through the 93rd Evacuation Hospital for a non-battle related injury, and invited me to visit him in Saigon if I ever got the chance. I took out my little book and gave him a call. I grabbed my shaving kit and 45 caliber pistol, then went to the motor pool to requisition a vehicle. Through a friend in the motor pool I was given a drivers license that stated I was authorized to drive any vehicle under five tons, despite never testing on any vehicle. Normally a jeep would be checked out for the short trip to Saigon, but I wanted to check out a two and a half ton, called a "Deuce and a Half". The reason? I thought it would be more fun to drive. By the time I got into Saigon I had the hang of driving the big truck, and it turned out to be a perfect vehicle choice for the busy streets. The streets of Saigon were completely filled with thousands of motor bikes and jitney's that clogged most of the intersections. Our military jeeps got bogged down in this heavy traffic also, but my choice of vehicle proved to be perfect. When I drove down the streets, the sea of motor bikes just parted and let me drive through. I didn't even have to blow the horn. I located the Liaison's building and found a place to park - basically any place that the truck would fit. The Liaison sergeant already had a plan for us to drive to a location near Quan Loi for some business he had to take care of, so we took his jeep. When he finished his business, he took me up the mountain to see the huge Buddha statue that had been built at the very top, and overlooked the surrounding valleys. I have no idea how this feat was accomplished, but was very impressive. I was glad to have visited what I viewed as a tourist attraction, but actually was a much visited holy site for Buddhists. It was strange that two American sergeants were on this mountaintop alone with civilian Vietnamese around us, and no explosive sounds or shooting heard. Was the war put on hold here? Don't know, don't care, it was great.

After my tour we headed back to Saigon to do some serious bar hopping. It certainly was different from going into a bar in the States. For one thing, the bars in the States frowned upon carrying a 45 Caliber pistol while ordering a drink. In the bar was different also, all of the patrons were men, both Americans as well as a few

South Vietnamese soldiers. Tending to these men were several gorgeous Vietnamese women dressed in their finest Vietnamese garments and makeup, and making their rounds among the men. When we sat down it only took moments before we had a couple of these ladies approach us. They wanted us to buy them a drink we called "Saigon Tea" (a drink just a little stronger than water) but the establishment charged the men a hefty price for the drink. The girls were not allowed to stay and talk with the men unless a Tea was purchased for them. This protocol didn't affect me because I didn't have enough money to buy anyone but myself a few beers. My sergeant partner didn't buy any drinks for them either, because he just knew better. As we sat there drinking a few beers and talking, the next phase of the bar girls took place. One of the girls came up to me and offered to buy her own Tea, just to be allowed to stand there and talk with me. I told her I didn't mind, because at this point I was getting curious. Well, you guessed it, her offer came pretty quick; she suggested a price to be able to go home with her for the night. When we wouldn't bite on the offer, she moved on to another potential income source. With that we finished our drinks and went back to his quarters to get some sleep. The following morning I got into my truck for the return trip to Long Binh appreciating my in-country mini-vacation.

Bob Hope, the actor, comedian and entertainer had been performing shows for the military since World War II, the Korean War, and now in Vietnam. He would only perform in large venues with usually a few gorgeous up and coming actresses, and other lesser known dancers or sport figures. While stationed at the 93rd Evacuation

Hospital bob Hope was scheduled to do one show the following day. As luck would have it I was tied up with my duties for most of the show, but was able to slip away and find a spot in the very back of the crowd to try and get a peek. A peek at the stage was all I got, and I tried to take a long range photo of a dance performance. That was all of the famous Bob Hope tour show I got to see.

As it turned out, not seeing much of the Bob Hope show wasn't a major disappointment, since a few days later Johnny Cash and his wife June Carter came into the Emergency Room when I was there. The patient was Johnny Cash, and he looked completely drained, his face and skin were chalk white, and looked bad. He had been performing somewhere in our area and was still wearing his heavy black stage coat he wore as his signature look. June Carter also had her performance dress on, and was made up to the "Nines". As soon as he was brought in everyone went into full action, removing the heavy outer clothes, and starting an IV. He was dehydrated, and suspected to have taken, but not proven, some type of enhancement drugs in preparation for his performance. Since the Cash's had only been in country a few days on a short tour, the intense heat and not enough water had taken him down. With the help of the IV he was able to rehydrate, and a couple of hours later he was released. His manager said he would remind them to stay hydrated until they left Vietnam. Being in the ER during the entire time, I was able too get autographs from them both while they were preparing to leave.

My year in country was coming to a conclusion, and that would make me "Short," or a short timer. My tour will be over, and my commitment of two years for active duty will also be fulfilled. Counting the days until the happens is still a couple of weeks away, and I haven't seen a replacement to train yet. I did get a visit from the Command Sergeant Major representing General Talbott. He told me the General wanted me to consider extending my requirement in the Army. He offered me a choice to be promoted to a Second Lieutenant or be promoted to a Sergeant First Class E-7, which would make me the youngest SFC E-7 in the entire Army. The offer was very enticing, but I had a plan when I decided to join the Army by volunteering for the Draft, and I planned to follow it. I thanked the Sergeant Major, but declined his generous offer. Unfortunately he was disappointed, I think he thought I was going to jump at the rank opportunity. We both stood up, and he said to stand at attention. His Aid handed him a box. It held a Bronze Star for Service, and he pinned it over my pocket, shook my hand and said, "Thank You for your service". Wow, so unexpected, and no awards ceremony - just a few other staff besides us were in the room. I walked back with him to his waiting helicopter, and when they flew off, I would not see anyone from Division again. What a ride I've had!

PARTY TIME

During my last week in Vietnam, the sergeants in my hootch decided to give me a going away party at our place, since we had the only patio and grill on the base. The base commander had a patio but was missing a grill. The date was set for two days before I was to leave country, and even though the party was for me, I was in charge of getting the meat for the grill. It was only fair. I had the contacts and cigarettes to trade, and trade I did. The Mess hall sergeant traded cigarettes for a case of New York steaks, and of course he was also invited to the party. My barrack buddies supplied the beer and hard liquor, and other types of food just showed up with the guests. Sergeant Tito brought a really large bowl of a rice recipe from his home country of Guam. It was a great party, that grew larger as each hour passed, and as loud as it got, the "MP's," Military Police never showed up to stop it.

The following day was slow and quiet, and Mamasan cleaned up for us as well. I spent the last day getting myself together to process out of the 93rd Evacuation Hospital, which didn't take long. I already had my orders that had been sent down from Division Headquarters. The jeep ride to Tan San Nhut was strange. After being in Vietnam for a year, and having been shot in the chest, this ride had me wondering if I would encounter a freak accident along the way. Or maybe shot to death by a sniper the last day in country. There had been stories of soldiers so close to going home, and then getting killed. Just superstitions, but things like that go through your mind. When I got to the airport, I actually ran into one of my school buddies from Crossland High School, Jack Lamay. What were the odds of running into someone I knew -slim, very slim. But when we approached each other, Jack had a shocked look on his face. He said he heard back home in the States that I had died. I assured him the rumors were wrong, but I did have a close call. We only had enough time to talk for a few minutes before we had to continue in our different directions. I found out later that Jack did make it back home safely.

Going to Vietnam last year we flew Trans World Airways, and we were treated like heroes. But now leaving the country I was getting ready to board a military aircraft that had us sitting on the floor in strap seats, packed like sardines, and facing towards the planes tail section. No luxury, and no flight service of food or drink, and we were flying all the way to the air base in Alaska, USA. It's going to be a long flight! We did change planes in Alaska, and we boarded a commercial jetliner to continue our flight to Seattle, Washington. A few hours later we landed at the airport. We were greeted by military personnel that took us to the processing center for the final time. We were issued any items of uniform we needed, got our discharge orders, and received our final pay - this time in American dollars!

STEAK AND MILK

What happened next was an unexpected very nice gesture. Some of the Seattle residents had formed a group to welcome soldiers returning from Vietnam, and take them to their homes for a night. Two of us were gathered up at the processing station to go home with a man and woman. I would have preferred to have gone to the airport and flown home, but they went through a lot of effort to provide a nice homecoming, and I decided to go along with the program. On the drive to their house we passed by Boeing, the largest US airplane manufacturer, and the man told us that was where he was employed. When we arrived at their house we were taken to our rooms to get settled. We had our showers and shaves and went downstairs. The dining room table was already set for dinner, and we all took our seats. At each place setting was a tall glass of milk, and a steak and baked potato on our plates. They made a big deal about the steak and milk, as if we hadn't had either over the past year. I don't know where they got that notion. I thought why should they know any different, so I didn't bust their bubble, and raved about having both, and thanked them profusely. They both had lots of questions for us, as if they were comparing the stories they had been hearing on the evening news. I don't know whether or not they were satisfied with our answers to their questions. We were both tired, so we turned in early. In the morning we had a quick breakfast with more milk, and they drove us to the airport. Nice couple of people.

Finally, I was on my plane heading home to the Baltimore airport. My mind was racing from everything that had happened during the previous days, and for the days to come. When my plane landed, I was met by my wife. I gathered up my duffle bag from the baggage pick up area, and drove to my parents house in Hillcrest Heights. On the way there I heard on the radio that earlier Neil Armstrong had become the first man to walk on the moon, and the Apollo 11 space mission was a success. Wow, that great moment in history was happening while I was still in the air coming home. I will never forget July 20, 1969. Arriving at the house, and walking up to the closed front door, I saw a full sized poster photo of me from basic training tacked to it. When I walked in everyone was there - relatives, friends, neighbors all yelling surprise. And it was. Another party! After being away a year, you would think my only wish would be to sneak off with my new wife and go to my newly furnished apartment, but I wanted to stay with the people at the party instead. I reasoned after a year apart, another few hours delay could be tolerated. Johnny was there, he got home only a couple of days earlier. He planned to go into the Nursing profession, and then to Medical Research and the National Institute of Health. Due to his eyesight he couldn't get his helicopter license, but has since gotten his fixed wing and helicopter licenses for his own pleasure. Mark also returned safely, and went into the hospitality business with the Marriott Corporation, and later opened a business performing building appraisals. Paul was also at the homecoming party. He went into the Education Field at Charles County Community College, and later became a counselor there. Frank became a store manager for Toys R Us, down in Virginia. I went back to the job held for me in the Elevator trade with General Elevator, and years later bought an elevator company of my own.

My buddies and I had come a long way from those lazy nights sitting around in a circle on lawn chairs. Did we solve all of life's questions we had then? Not yet. That is still a work in progress.

EPILOGUE

Life is like a book about roller-coasters, with many chapters depicting many events, each affecting the next. At times bringing you down to the depths of the bottom, so far you think you will never be able to crawl out, but you do. And there are times you soar to new heights where you feel you are at the top of the world and there are no limits. We all experience these highs and lows in varying degrees throughout life. What you do with these opportunities is what separates us from one another. When you're at the top of your game and taking a dive toward the bottom, throw your arms up above your head and enjoy the ride, because you won't be at the bottom long.

I was fortunate to have been dealt the hand with an over abundance of the highs, and for that I am thankful. You need to have visited the lows before you can realize when you reach a high.

PHOTOGRAPHS

Chinook

M-60 Machine Gun Range

Some of my 1/2 "Dracula" men

After graduation from Basic

Machine gun M-60 Range
The one on the right is me, firing the M-60 for the demonstration to both companies

Chinook retrieving downed helicopter

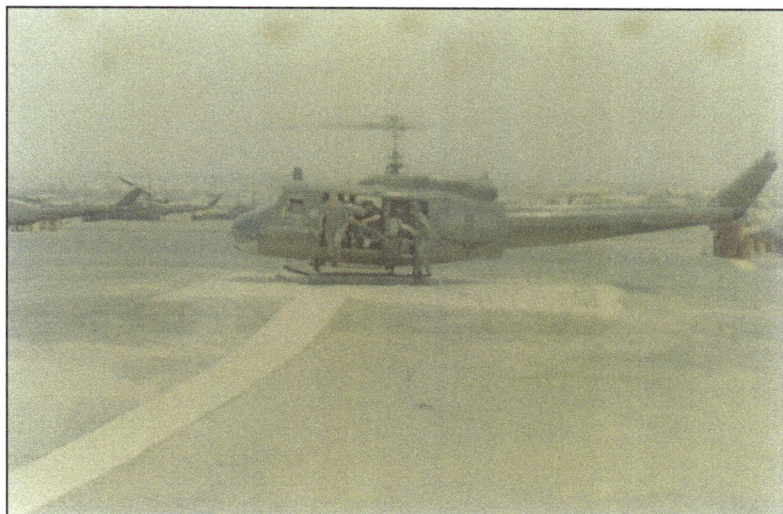

1st Division Sgt. Major arriving at 93rd EVAC

Small group of my men at Base Camp

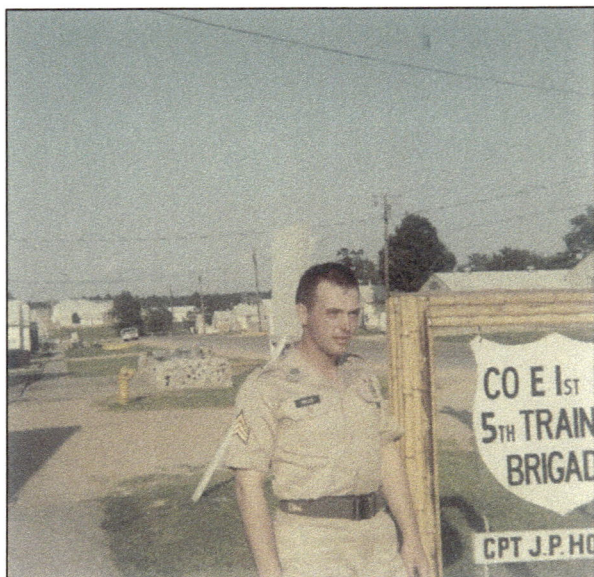

Training at Fort Polk as a new Sgt E-5

1st Division a Headquarters Di AN

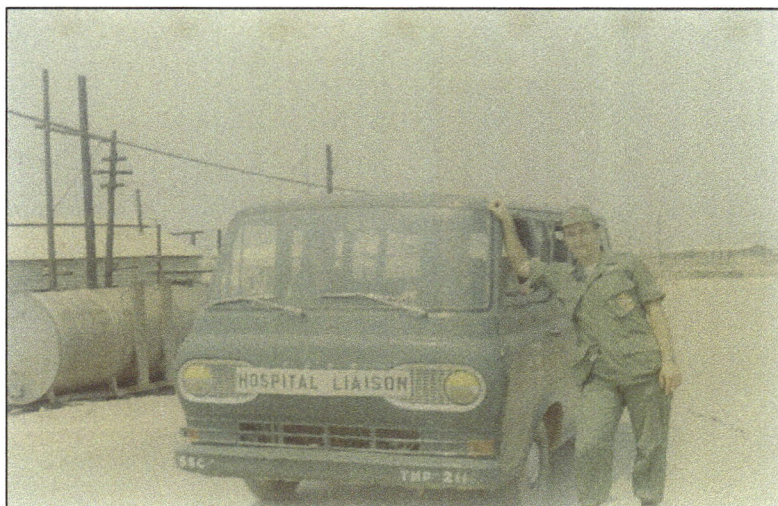

Me with the other Liason's van

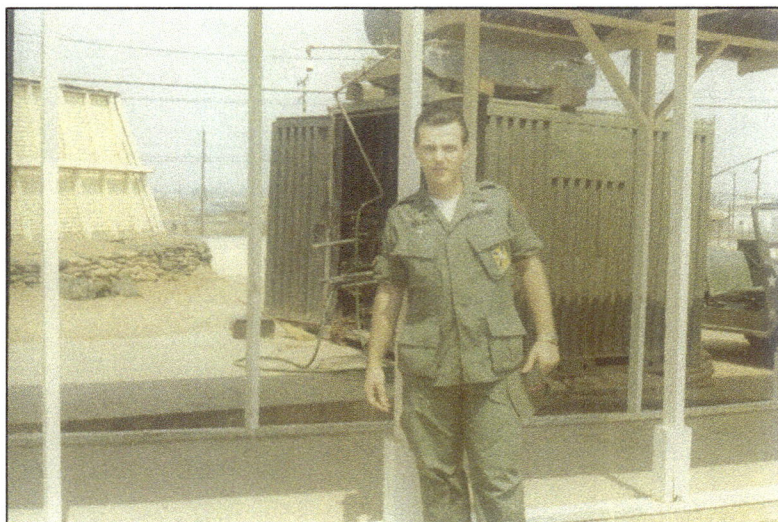

Standing outside Emergency Room
as Liason at 93rd EVAC

H-1D Medical Helicopter

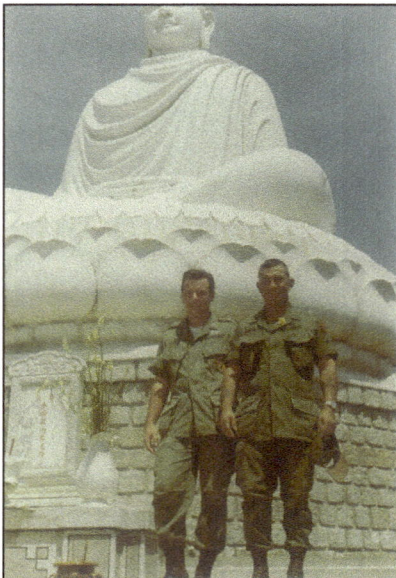

Near Quan Loi with my liason friend

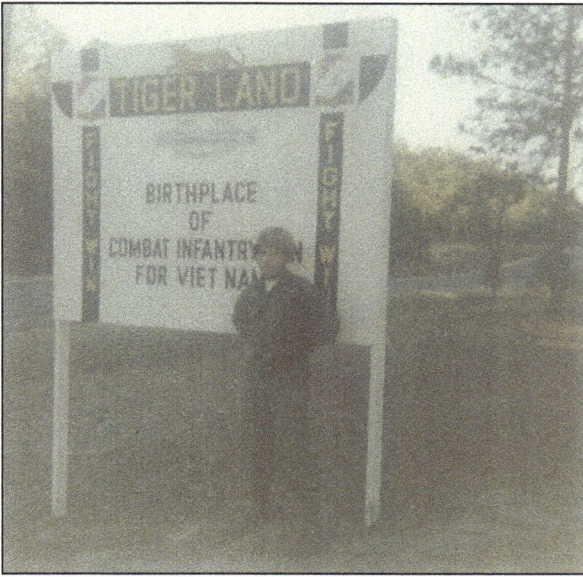

AIT Training at Fort Polk

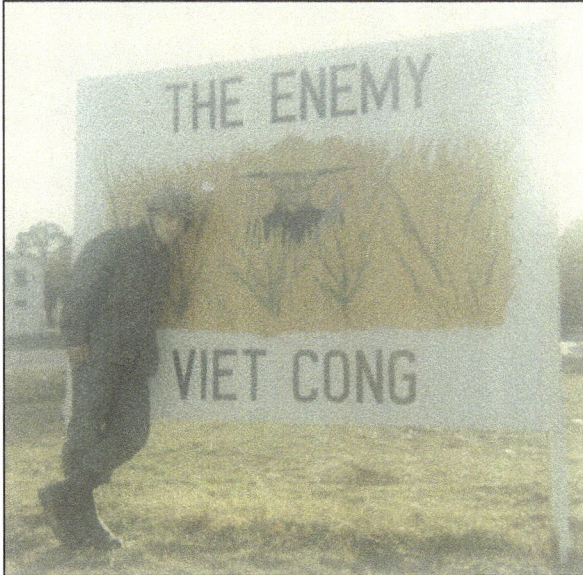

AIT Training at Fort Polk

Me on right with one of my men at Base Camp

**Our hootch at 93rd EVAC
with water tank, patio, and privacy fence**

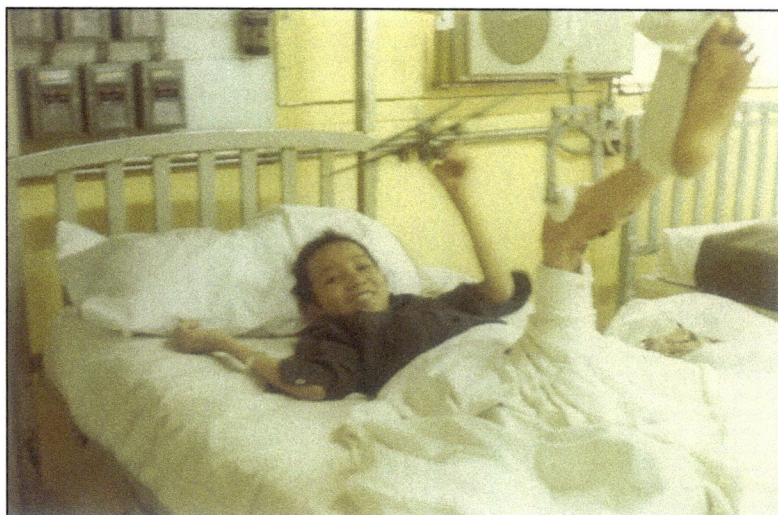

The wounded Vietnamese boy I gave a haircut

NO MISSION TOO DIFFICULT | NO | SACRIFICE TOO GREAT | DUTY FIR

1st Division Base at Lai Khe

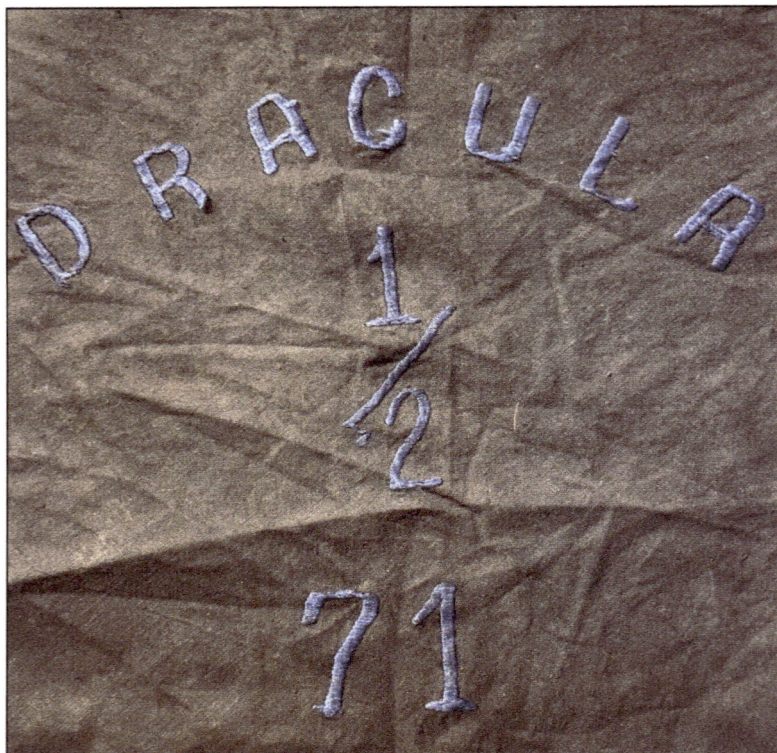

My Silk 1/2 Black Scarf "Dracula"

Johnny Cash and June Carter

Rocky Marciano - Prize Fighter

Sebastian Cabot - Actor

"Request your assistance to get me a personal copy of the very elaborate and outstanding blue folder containing the "certificate of combat awards."

Joseph D. Buda, Command Sergeant Major
627th Hospital Center, APO 96343 Japan

"Sergeant Major Walls commented about the excellent care he received there and the outstanding service you were providing."

Robert C. Dalehite, Command Sergeant Major
106th General Hospital

"Staff Sergeant Myles has identified himself very closely with the patients from the 1st Infantry Division and constantly assisted them and insured that their needs are taken care of. He likewise has voluntarily learned a tremendous amount of patient care and willingly accepts additional responsibilities associated with the hospital in addition to providing outstanding support for his men."

Robert N. Grant, MAJ, MC
Chief of Surgery

"The work that SSG Myles has performed here has contributed greatly to the morale and speedier recovery of the 1st Infantry Division personnel admitted to the hospital."

Cesar A. Lopez, COL, MC
Commanding

"Your performance of duty in this challenging position has been truly exemplary; this has been noted and commented upon by the hospital staff, the patients, and visitors as well. You are providing an invaluable service for which I extend my appreciation and congratulations."

Orwin C. Talbott, Major General, USA
Commanding - 1st Division

www.ingramcontent.com/pod-product-compliance
Lightning Source LLC
Chambersburg PA
CBHW051214090426
42742CB00022B/3449

* 9 7 8 1 6 2 8 0 6 2 6 4 9 *